Ulrike Müller

Cats

Caring for Them
Feeding Them
Understanding Them

Photographs: Monika Wegler
Drawings: Renate Holzner

C O N T E N T S

3 Understanding Your Pet and Keeping It Occupied

What You Need

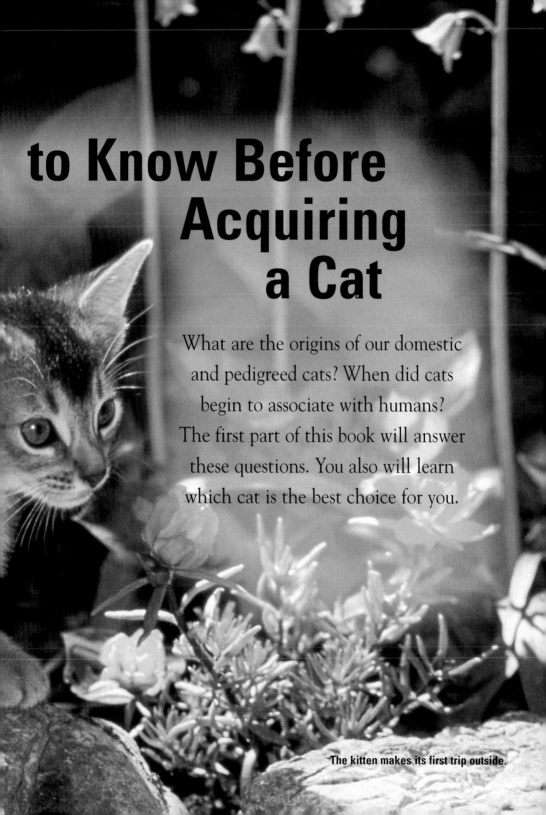

to Know Before Acquiring a Cat

What are the origins of our domestic and pedigreed cats? When did cats begin to associate with humans? The first part of this book will answer these questions. You also will learn which cat is the best choice for you.

The kitten makes its first trip outside.

Cats—Tales from Their Past

A twelve-week-old Persian kitten. This breed comes originally from Asia Minor.

Venerated, pampered, tolerated, and persecuted—in i 4,000-year history of assoc ation with mankind, th domestic cat has experience the entire gamut of shifts human opinion.

Cats Conquer the Earth

Wild cats live in almost parts of the world. Over th course of millions of year evolution has shaped the into perfect hunters—pre ators who overwhelm the prey in a surprise attack. Wi their keen senses, highly de eloped intelligence, strengt stamina, and agility, the b cats have won a position superiority within the anim kingdom.

A small cat from Nor Africa, the Libyan wild cat Nubia (*Felis lybica*), came terms with humankind abo 4,000 years ago. Domest cats are descended from th ancestor.

Today, relatively indepen ent, free-living populations domestic cats are comm throughout the world. A gre

High above on the observation point is a wild-colored Abyssinian cat. This is one of the oldest breeds.

variety of breeds are bred by the millions and kept in our homes as beloved, well-cared-for pets.

When Cats Formed an Attachment to Humans

Some 4,000 years have elapsed since the cat discovered its "love" for humans. Much evidence supports the hypothesis that domestic cats were known first in the Near East and came to Europe by way of Greece. The older and better-

known theory states that the cat's origin lies in Egypt. Perhaps both theories are true.

The Libyan Wild Cat. It has been proved that the Libyan wild cat, which was very common in North Africa, was held in high esteem by the ancient Egyptians. The Libyan wild cat is slender and has large ears and a long tail. Its coat has light-colored stripes as well as spotted patterns.

The relationship between cat and man developed on the

9

basis of mutual benefit in Egypt's highly advanced ancient civilization. Cats found an embarrassment of riches in the granaries of the people on the Nile. The cats sharply reduced the mouse and rat population attracted by the grain. Consequently, the cats earned the profound regard of the ancient Egyptians. For a while, their beauty, elegance, and independent behavior led the Egyptians to worship them as goddesses.

How the Cat Became Domesticated

The process of domestication took place gradually. It may have started with cats that were tamer than others, who found living close to humans thoroughly agreeable. When such cats produced offspring, the kittens delighted many cat lovers. Over time, as humans were in close contact with cats and provided for them, the process of selection increasingly favored especially tame animals.

The Romans Brought Them to Europe

When Romans spread the Egyptian domestic cats throughout Europe, the domestic cats may have coupled occasionally with the wild cats of the forest (*Felis silvestris*). Because the nature of the wild animal is dominant in the young kittens from such matings, they usually cannot be tamed. Therefore, despite the biological possibility of interbreeding between the two species, the genes of the European forest cats are not likely to have been passed on to our domestic cats, even over a long period of time. Young wild cats with the augmented hereditary factors of a domestic cat would be unable to survive in the wild. This is why the two courses of evolution remained separate.

Both Goddess and Witch

The cat has not always been cherished by all people all the time. Some admire their beauty and like cats precisely because of their independent nature. Others have an uncomfortable feeling about them and think they seem "fake."

At the beginning of the cat's association

The short-haired cat stretches its paw forward, makes a little wave, and purrs at the same time—a clear sign of contentment.

s opposed to youngsters f true wildcats, young omesticated cats have n inherited facility for a ertain tameness.

with humans, the ancient Egyptians accorded it goddess status. The Egyptians depicted Bastet, the goddess of femininity and maternity and the spouse of the sun god Ra, with the head of a cat. Like human corpses, thousands of cats were embalmed after death, wrapped in strips of cloth, and laid to rest in specially prepared burial chambers.

Initially people in Europe marveled at and admired the first specimens of the domestic cat. Their rarity earned them great esteem. Quite soon, however, their high fertility rate resulted in an enormous increase in their numbers. As they spread, they were tolerated as destroyers of vermin but were often treated with cruelty. The unwanted offspring were often placed in a sack and drowned in the nearest stream or in the village pond. The populace considered cats, like dogs, a welcome addition to their daily bill of fare.

When religious mania blossomed once more during the Middle Ages, cats came in for their share of the suffering. Possessed by a belief in witchcraft, people suddenly began to view cats as demonic beings controlled by Satan.

Frequently cats became the companions of older women living alone, who took loving care of them. For centuries such women were regarded as witches and persecuted. The Roman Catholic Pope and the Inquisition mandated that they be burned with their cats. It was not until the seventeenth century that popular opinion in Europe gradually swung in the cats' favor.

As in Egypt, however, cats always enjoyed great esteem in other parts of the world, under the religions of Islam and Buddhism. In East Asia, China, and Japan, for example, cats were venerated, and they enjoyed the status of pampered pets.

A frisky kitty trio: They climb up the tree daringly. Now how are they going to get down?

TIP

If you are planning to purchase a pedigreed cat you should first visit several cat shows. That way you can get an accurate picture of the different breeds and the preferred breed standards (see p. 36). You might even find a kitten there being offered for sale.

The Cat Today

The results of fairly recent behavioral research have led us to an improved understanding of the cat's nature and needs.

Advances in veterinary medicine and increased efforts to prevent cruelty to animals are helping to check the misery resulting from uncontrolled reproduction by cats. Vaccinations protect cats against contagious diseases.

The number of cats living in houses or apartments with people has increased substantially and is apparently still on the rise. Similarly, the organized breeding of pedigreed cats is constantly increasing.

On Domestic and Pedigreed Cats

Many different cat breeds have appeared. Some breeds are descended from domestic cats that lived outdoors; however, most breeds were bred and crossed from mutations that occurred by chance (for example, if a litter included an especially long-haired animal, it was used for further breeding).

In some cases, features that would really be considered genetic defects were also used to create a breed. In this way, for example, serious health problems arose in a Persian variety bred in America, the so-called Peke-faced Persian. These animals, which have almost no facial cranium, suffer from difficulty in breathing, tearing eyes, and problems with food ingestion. In some countries there now are laws that prohibit the breeding of such "nuisance breeds."

Most pedigreed cats, though, are extremely beautiful animals that have retained much of the original elegance of the wild cat. Their grace usually goes hand in hand with lovable traits and human-centered behavior.

The seven-week-old kitten deftly leaps after its prey.

Which Cat Is Right for You?

Cats are independent pe sonalities that do n always comply with the wish of "their" human. Once y accept that fact, you will ha a good basis for a harmonio relationship with your pet.

The Nature of the Cat

First it's important to look the way of life of our domest cat's ancestor, the Libyan wi cat of North Africa.

The Libyan wild cat liv largely alone in its territo The cat must find the enough nourishment a places for retreat and res Since other cats compete f these fundamentals of lif their presence in the territo is not tolerated; they a driven away—except duri the season of mating a rearing young.

Domestic and purebr cats also continue to carry t legacy of their wild ancesto Their hunting instinct a their drive to defend the territory, however, are longer so well developed.

Cats are distinctive individua Even offspring of the same lit develop different personal characteristics.

Do Cats Like Music?

Music, if it is played softly, will not disturb your cat. But if you play your music at full blast, the cat will not like it at all—just as little as it likes any scream or loud noise. Cats have a much better sense of hearing than we humans. Your cat can hear tones that you can no longer hear. When a rolled up ball of paper drops rustling to the floor, the cat knows exactly where to look for it. It has such finely developed ears that it can distinguish the patter of mouse paws from other sounds in its vicinity.

Now, perhaps, you have some sense of how much your cat suffers from loud noises. You may be able to understand why it will leave the room suddenly, and you will not be able to find it for the next few hours.

Because of a specifically inherited tendency, many domestic and pedigreed cats display the behavioral patterns of young cats well into old age. This fact makes it possible for them to develop a distinct social bond with their "chosen" humans. Nevertheless, to develop a good relationship with the animal and give it a happy life, a cat lover must keep in mind the "wild heritage" of his or her pet.

What a Cat Expects of You

Outdoor domestic cats and cats that are allowed outdoors regularly can satisfy many of their natural requirements without human assistance. Indoor cats, however, need special attention.

An indoor cat, for example, loves to live in a home that allows it room to play and explore and provides a number of places where it can hide or rest in comfort (see drawing, pages 54–55). Naturally, for purely indoor cats it is especially important to supply cat food, fresh drinking water, a scratching post, and a litter box (see page 48).

All cats like to spend quiet time cuddling. Young animals in particular need extensive periods of play, preferably with you. Alternatively, you can encourage your pet to play with a toy (see page 51).

Fundamental changes in their sphere of life are not welcomed by cats. Such changes include, for example, moving to another house, rearranging or remodeling

15

your home, or barring your pet from rooms that previously were accessible to it.

Cats detest noise. Therefore, be sure to put your cat safely indoors on the Fourth of July, for example. Frequently cats have disappeared after the Fourth of July.

Cats spend a great part of their day dozing and sleeping. Their health will suffer in the long run if they are disturbed repeatedly at these times.

Unsuitable methods of training frequently result in failure, and they can place considerable stress on the relationship between cat and human (see Training, page 104).

Training programs that can succeed with dogs are doomed to fail with cats. They themselves decide when they will do something. They cannot be forced to do anything.

Cats are often quite forbearing with others of their kind, and sometimes real friendships will even develop between cats that are well acquainted with each other (see Getting Cats Used to One Another, page 100). Keeping too many cats in a limited space, however, creates stress for each individual; stress makes a cat aggressive and susceptible to illness.

It is by no means a foregone conclusion that cats will get used to each other. A cat is particularly displeased when another cat is set down "under its nose" in its accustomed sphere. It views the new cat as an interloper and behaves in a correspondingly rejective fashion. That can also be true where other unfamiliar animals and humans are concerned (see Cats and Other Pets, page 101).

Let Your Preference be the Deciding Factor

People who like cats usually entertain friendly feelings for all species and breeds. Nevertheless, preferences differ when it comes to getting your own cat.

To help you choose the cat that's best for you, I have listed in the following table the differences that characterize the temperaments of the individual cat breeds. I have also presented special pointers on keeping each of these breeds. The data are based on surveys of breeders and cat owners. However, you need to keep in mind that cats are very definite individuals. Each cat develops its own independent, unique personality.

T I P

If you want to acquire pedigreed cat, it is adv able to take out insuran on the cat. This can h defray the costs of the v erinarian and/or in the ca of a loss can replace value of the animal.

For the damage persons and to objects) th your cat causes, your n mal comprehensive insu ance might pay.

A five-week-old male kitter with typical baby blue eyes that will later change their color.

e Abyssinian climbs the tree
ınk elegantly. This cat needs
ts of activities and attention.

The Different Types of Cats

Breed	Character Traits
Abyssinian	High-spirited, sensitive, devoted, affectionate, and soft-voiced, the Abyssinian needs a great deal of activity and attention (see page 38).
Balinese	Bred from Siamese stock, Balinese are intelligent, imaginative, often bold, and insistently devoted. They are the "gymnasts" of the purebreds and have a great need for exercise.
Birman	With shining blue eyes, Birmans need much love and are strongly fixated on humans. Their well-balanced temperament is a successful synthesis of Siamese and Persian traits (see page 40).
Chartreuse	Called "British shorthairs," Chartreuse are easy-going and robust, like cuddling, and are not demanding or stubborn. They love children and are easy to care for (see page 39).
Chinchilla	The Chinchilla and Silver-shaded (both color variants of the true Persians) are not sensitive but are playful, devoted, high-spirited, and well balanced. They have green eyes and a white coat with the tips of their hairs colored.
Domestic (House) Cat	Well suited for life as indoor or indoor-outdoor cat, this cat is heavily dependent on life with humans for its character development.

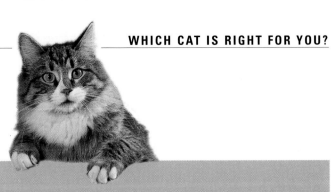

Breed	Character Traits
Havana	This extravagant brown Oriental cat with green eyes is a pet for people with good "cat sense." It needs much attention.
Himalayan/ Color Point	This cat has the vivacity of the Siamese and the calm disposition of the Persian. It is not suited for keeping outdoors because of its long coat.
Maine Coon	A dignified, independent breed of cat that can easily be kept outdoors, the Maine Coon is considered lovable, smart, and agile (see page 42).
Norwegian Forest	This active, freedom-loving cat loves children, is sociable, and loves the outdoors in any weather. It is not suited for a small apartment (see page 43).
Persian	Persians are said to be the most placid of the purebred cats. This cat's need for exercise depends largely on its age. Their hunting instinct is not very pronounced (see page 44).
Rex	An intelligent, charming cat for people with a taste for the unusual, the Rex is lively and uncomplicated. Since Rex cats have only a thin coat, they need to be kept indoors.
Siamese	The Siamese is one of the oldest and most popular breeds. Select this breed only if you are a cat lover who can devote plenty of time and attention to your pet (see page 45).
Somali	In coat color and disposition, the Somali resembles the Abyssinian. It is sweet, loving, devoted, friendly. All it needs is a room with a view.

Considerations Before Acquiring a Cat

Whether you have let a stray kitten into your heart or have decided to purchase a cat, you need to consider a few fundamental issues first.

Decision Making Aids:

1 Many people are allergic to cat hair. Are you sure that neither you nor any other member of your family has such a reaction (see Important Note, page 127)?

2 The average life span of a cat is 15 to 20 years. During that period of time, you are responsible for a living creature. Do you realize what that entails?

3 Just filling the cat's food and water dishes and keeping the litter box clean is not enough. Along with feeding, the daily "chat and cuddle time" with you is of enormous importance for the cat. Only in that way can a harmonious relationship between you and your pet develop over time (see Getting the Cat Settled Properly, p. 98). Single people who work in the daytime and always keep their pet indoors face more demands. The cat longs for "its" person to come home. Then little time remains for leisure activities and interests outside the home.

Singles who work may wish to acquire two cats at the same time—ideally, litter mates, because they are already close playmates. They will settle in quickly and will certainly not suffer from boredom.

4 Coat care is more time-consuming for long-haired cats than for short-haired ones (see Grooming is Not Just Beautifying, page 66).

5 Do you have lots of patience? Young kittens can get into a great deal of mischief. They climb up the curtains, dig in flowerpots, chew on plants, knock vases over, and leave scratch marks on all the upholstery and wallpaper. You can expect to find cat hairs on your furniture, carpets, and clothes and sometimes in your soup as well. Cats sometimes vomit hair balls or fail to do their "business" in the litter box.

Domestic or Purebred Cat?

In terms of their disposition and behavior, there are no great differences between domestic cats and purebreds.

o young and already so
urious: Norwegian Forest
ttens by their first
connaissance in the garden.

There is a widespread belief that a purebred doesn't "want to go outdoors." But the yearning to get outdoors does not depend on the breed. It is wrong to assume that "ordinary" domestic cats are "wilder" than purebreds. Purebred cats can also be kept as outdoor pets, just as domestic cats can be kept exclusively indoors.

Financial Expenditures

Costs of Acquisition. Domestic farm kittens are often available free. Such a kitten will not have been wormed and vaccinated; a checkup at the veterinarian's office is definitely advisable (see page 72).

You may be expected to pay for having a kitten from an animal shelter spayed or neutered and vaccinated. (Some shelters provide these services free of charge. Check with the individual shelter to find out what it will and will not provide [see page 31].)

Buying a pedigreed cat is expensive. Count on spending several hundred dollars. The prices vary considerably, since

One heart and one soul: Tenderly the boy pets his Siamese cat who is visibly enjoying it.

22

Can Cats See Colors?

For a long time people assumed that cats could see only gray tones. In the meantime we have learned that they can distinguish between some colors: for example, red and green or yellow and blue. Colors do not play a major role in a cat's life. A cat's eye orients itself to light and dark. It acts like a camera. In bright sunshine the pupils contract; at dusk they expand and catch even the tiniest glimpse of light. In this way your cat sees about six times better than you do. Cats can also "hear" with their eyes. Cats' eyes have nerve cells that transmit to the brain sounds that the ears no longer perceive. That's how even blind cats can catch flies.

different breeds go for different prices and a distinction is made between pet-quality and show-quality animals.

Equipment Costs. These expenses depend more on your personal tastes than on the cat's requirements.

Food Costs. You can expect to spend $30 to $60 per month.

Veterinary Costs. At least once a year, there will be required vaccinations. You should consider the possibility that your cat might fall ill and have to be taken to the veterinarian.

Keeping a Cat in a Rented Apartment

Before you buy or adopt a cat, look at your lease. If there is any doubt whether pets are allowed in your building, you should get the landlord's written permission to keep a cat (see The Law and the Cat Owner, page 26).

In poorly soundproofed apartments the howls of a female cat in heat can become a source of disturbance for your neighbors. Having your pet neutered or spayed will remedy the situation (see page 82).

Male or Female?

Differences in Disposition. I have never noticed any gender-dependent differences in my cats' dispositions. Whether a cat is relatively wild, gentle, friendly, or shy depends on its individual personality (see pages 18–19).

Sex-specific Differences. Unaltered males (tomcats) and females have pronounced sexual behavior. During mating season, the female becomes restless and meows almost non-stop. If her desire for a male is not satisfied, she rolls around on the floor, emitting loud cries (see page 84).

The male shows his readiness to mate by "spraying" (see page 84). If he has an opportunity to get outdoors, he roams far and wide, stays away from home for nights on end, and does battle with other males to win the favor of a female.

Spaying or neutering a cat eliminates its sex drive. Neutered males and spayed females often form a particularly close bond with their owners.

Whether a house cat or pedigreed, both bear the legacy of their ancestors. Every cat enjoys strolling through its own territory.

T I P

Before a cat moves in with you, it should be at least eight weeks old. If it is separated from its mother much earlier, it is likely to be sickly and frequently lag behind in its development. A pedigree kitten, therefore, should be passed on to its new owner only after twelve weeks.

A Cat as a Playmate?

A cat is not a good playmate for a small child. The child is too young to comprehend the independent nature of the cat, and the cat will certainly use its claws to defend itself against any rough handling.

Things are different if the cat was already there and a baby now is on the way. There is no reason to get rid of the cat. The child and the cat quickly will learn to respect each other and to show mutual consideration. From the very outset, parents need to teach their child the proper way to treat the cat.

Older children often hit it off very well with a cat. They are capable of understanding the cat and taking its needs into consideration. The cat will have a positive influence on the child's development: he or she will learn to accept responsibility, to develop a sense of duty, and to be considerate.

Vacationing—With or Without Your Cat?

If you take a few things into account when planning your trip, a vacation with a cat is possible. For example, your destination should not be too distant. Long car trips, train trips, or exhausting flights are stressful for a cat. If you want to spend your vacation abroad with your cat, find out ahead of time what entry regulations apply to animals. Your veterinarian or the consulate of the country in question can give you information.

If you would like to take a vacation without it, staying at home in the cat's customary environment with a sitter is easiest on your pet. You need to line up someone ahead of time to look after the cat. Addresses might be found in the local section of your daily newspaper.

Carefully scrutinize petboarding facilities ahead of time. For a cat, separation from its home and its owner involves great psychological stress. Its susceptibility to disease is increased by the situation. It is especially important that it has all its vaccinations beforehand. Some facilities of this kind will accept only neutered male cats.

This long-haired kitten is always ready to play.

25

The Law and the Cat Owner

Community life depends on mutual considerations so that the cat lover living in a rented home in a community setting may expect consideration for his love of animals. On the other hand, the cat keeper should also have consideration for his neighbors before getting a cat.

Before you decide to get a cat, you should read over your lease. If there is any doubt whether pets are allowed in your building, it is advisable to get written permission from your landlord. If sound travels easily in the building, you should keep in mind that the loud meowing of a cat in heat can be a considerable nuisance for your neighbors.

The Owner's Responsibilities

The animal owner is responsible if a person is killed, injured, or something is damaged because of his animal (e.g., through biting, tearing clothes, injuring or killing other animals, etc.). It is therefore advisable to review your homeowner's or renter's insurance policy to see what extent you are covered in the event of such an incident.

Animal Protection Laws

Although the animal is still often classified by lawmakers as a "thing," there are some laws that protect the animal. No one may cause a pet pain, injury, or harm. Included here is the failure to feed an animal or to feed it enough. Under threat of compensatory fine, one is forbidden to abandon an animal.

Indoor Versus Outdoor Cats

Some people insist on letting their cats roam freely because they believe that depriving cats of their outdoor freedom is cruel. Most humane educators disagree, for many good reasons. Cats kept indoors live longer, healthier lives because they are less likely to be exposed to diseases, plagued by parasites, hit by cars, attacked by dogs, bitten by wild animals, caught in wild animal traps, poisoned by pesticides, and harmed by cruel people. By keeping your cat indoors, you will have fewer veterinary bills related to injuries from cat fights and similar mishaps. In

addition, you will have pea of mind, knowing that yo well-kept indoor cat has litt chance of contracting a disea or parasite that could be trar mitted to you or your family. long as you provide love ar attention, your cat will l quite happy and well-adjust living indoors. If you feel yo cat must experience the ou doors, supervise outings in tl yard, build an outdoor exerc run, or install a cat flap th provides safe access to screened-in porch. You can al teach your cat to walk on a leas but never tie a cat outdoc unattended; that's dangerous

Pet Identification

Cats allowed outdoors som times stray too far from hon and then can't find their w. back. Even cats kept indoc occasionally escape and g lost in unfamiliar territory. F these reasons, and becau some people steal pets for sa to research laboratories, yo cat is safer if it wears some so of identification.

Tattooing: While tattooir won't prevent your cat fro being lost or stolen, a pe manent ID may enhance i hances of recovery. Many laboratories will not buy a tattooed animal, and most shelters look for tattoos. A painless procedure provided by many veterinarians, tattooing involves inking the owner's Social Security number or a special code on the rear inner thigh. For best results, keep the area shaven and register the tattoo with a nationwide pet protection service that has a 24-hour hotline for tracing the number and finding the owner, no matter where the cat is found.

Collars and tags: These can be lost or removed, but they are better than nothing. A cat collar needs to have a stretch elastic or a breakaway section, so the animal can escape without choking if the collar catches on some object.

Like collars, ear tags embedded in the ear like a tiny earring are better than no ID at all, but they, too, can be cut off, ear and all, by desperate, unscrupulous pet thieves.

Microchips: Shelters in some areas use microchip technology to reunite lost pets with their owners. With this ID system, a veterinarian injects a tiny microchip under the skin between the cat's shoulder blades. The chip reflects radio waves emitted by a hand-held scanner that reads the chip's code number. The owner registers the code number in a computer database for tracking. Ask your veterinarian if this system is available in your area.

Licensing Your Cat

Although few states mandate cat licensing, it is advisable to license your cat. There are several benefits to this.

If your cat is lost and picked up by an animal shelter or pound, and it is not licensed or does not have an ID tag, your chances of seeing your cat again are slim. Animal shelters and pounds in many states will not hold an unlicensed cat as long as they will hold a cat wearing a tag. In some cities, pounds are not required to hold a cat at all, and stray cats not wearing identification are euthanized at once. To a degree, then, licensing would give cats legal recognition and, to some degree, it would give cat owners the right to demand certain considerations because their licensing fees would generate revenue.

Cats love to run free.

27

In addition to benefiting the owners of lost cats—not to mention the cats themselves, license fees would allow cat owners to help subsidize shelter activities, which dog owners, through their license fees, have been helping to subsidize for some time.

The Contract of Sale

Everyone who purchases a cat enters into a sales contract with the seller. Although this contract does not have to be drawn up in written form, since oral contracts are legally valid as well, a written sales contract is advisable, especially where valuable pedigreed cats are concerned. The animal should be described in detail (age, breed, sex, color), the pedigree papers should be produced, and the purchase price should be stated. If the seller expressly guarantees certain characteristics (pure-bred, neutered or spayed, etc.), you should make a written record of these assurances in the contract. If the assurances prove false, the buyer has the right to return the animal and receive a full refund.

A contract should also allow a new owner a definite period of time, usually three to five working days, in which to take the cat to a veterinarian for an examination. If the vet discovers any preexisting conditions such as leukemia or feline infectious peritonitis, you should have the right to return the animal at the seller's expense and to have the purchase price refunded.

If you give a breeder a deposit on a kitten, you should write "deposit for thus-and-such kitten" on the memo line of the check. You should make a similar notation when writing a check for the balance of the payments and find out in advance—and in writing if you wish—whether a deposit is refundable should you decide not to take the kitten. Remember, too, that once a breeder has accepted money or some other consideration in return for reserving a kitten for you, that breeder has entered into an option contract; and he or she cannot legally revoke or renegotiate the offer—as some breeders have been known to do—if the kitten turns out to be much better than the breeder had anticipated.

Be sure to read a contract meticulously before signing it because contracts are legal binding once they have be signed by both parties. If contract contains any stipu tions that you do not unde stand or do not wish to agr to—like a stipulation sayin that the cat can never declawed—you should disc these issues with the breed before signing.

In addition to the pedigre new owners may recei "papers" when they buy pedigreed cat. These pape usually consist of a registratio slip that the new owner c fill out and send—along wi the required $6 or $7 fee— the administrative office the association in which th kitten's litter has been reg tered. The association the returns a certificate of owne ship to the new owners.

Anyone who buys a kitt or a cat that already has be registered by its breeder w receive an owner's certifica On the back of that certi cate is a transfer-of-ownersh section that must be signed the breeder and the ne owner. Once the required si natures are present, the ne owner mails the certifica with the appropriate transf fee, to the administrati fice of the association in hich the cat has been regis- red. The association will nd back a new, amended rtificate of ownership to the w owner(s).

Many breeders will not ovide a registration slip to yone who buys a pet-quality tten until they receive proof at the kitten has been utered or spayed. Some eeders do not supply gistration slips on pet- ality kittens at all. Breeders thhold papers to prevent scrupulous people from ying a kitten at a pet price d then breeding it and to event the use of pet-quality ttens in breedings that ve virtually no chance of ntributing to the aesthetic provement of a breed.

Health Certificates

The most important docu- ments that accompany a kitten to its new home are health records and vaccination certificates. You should not accept a kitten without these papers. Some breeders, espec- ially those who produce a large number of kittens, economize by giving vaccina- tions themselves. There is nothing illegal about this prac- tice, yet there is more to immu- nizing a kitten than drawing vaccine into a syringe, inser- ting the needle under a kitten's skin, and pushing the plunger. Few, if any, breeders are capable of examining a kitten

as thoroughly as a veterinarian can before administering a vaccination. Indeed, a vaccin- ation is only as good as the examination that precedes it. This examination is important because vaccine given to a sick kitten will do more harm than good. Thus, a kitten should be examined by a veterinarian at least once before it is sold, pref- erably before its first vaccina- tion. Finally, all kittens being shipped should be accompan- ied by a health certificate issued by a veterinarian and by a certificate verifying that the kitten has received all the vaccinations required by the city or state to which the kit- ten is being shipped.

Especially when it comes to expensive pedigreed cats such as this Oriental short-haired cat, a written bill of sale is recommended.

Where to Get a Cat

Sometimes a cat will choo its own owner. But if y are purposefully looking fo suitable kitten, you have variety of possibilities.

A Barnyard Cat

Most farms have a cat. If th are not spayed or neuter they often have unwant offspring (see Neutering Spaying, page 82). Someo will gladly give you one of t kittens from the litter.

What to Keep in Mind. H does the mother cat beha toward humans? Does she wild or quite tame?

A mother cat who lead relatively independent life a does not bring her offspri down from the hayloft ur they are several weeks old w probably have very shy kitte that will take a long time become tame—if ever (s Problems and How to Sol Them, page 112).

If the cat lives in the hou however, the mother cat w also raise her young close her human family. Then t little creatures will already

Sometimes a cat will search itself for a place where it ca feel at home.

kitten from a farm could feel ry shy if it didn't live in the use there.

accustomed to humans, and a kitten from such a litter will quickly settle into your household as well.

Cats from the Animal Shelter

In municipal animal shelters, the cat cages in particular are always overcrowded. You are certain to find a cat there just for you.

Formalities at the Shelter. Animal shelters prefer to send their adult cats to new homes first. They are already wormed, vaccinated, and spayed or neutered. Usually you have to pay the vaccinations' cost and affirm that you will keep the cat only as an indoor pet.

A very young kitten is not yet ready to be spayed or neutered. Many shelters give you a certificate to defray the cost of the operation to be performed at a later date.

The Foundling

A cat from another neighborhood may choose your house as the new center of its life. Possibly the foundling will stir your heart, and you will decide to provide it with food, at least for the time being.

What to Keep in Mind. A little animal of this kind needs a new, permanent home. There are always people who are willing to feed such cats in their yard but refuse all responsibility and make no effort to develop a relationship with the animal. That doesn't help the foundling. Either look for a new home for the cat or decide to keep the cat permanently.

A Pedigreed Cat

Pet Store. If you are considering buying a pedigreed cat from a pet store, you should ask the pet shop owner for the name, address, and phone number of the animal's breeder. This will allow you to investigate the kitten's background before buying it.

If the pet shop owner is unwilling or unable to provide that information, you should proceed with caution because you will have less information about the kitten than would be available if the kitten was being purchased directly from its breeder.

The little kittens will be decisively molded by their mother. If she has a trust in humans, she will pass it on to her children.

Can Cats Dream?

Take time to observe your cat carefully when it is sleeping. Does it jerk its paws or the tip of the tail? Do the ears tremor lightly? Then it's probably dreaming. Sometimes it will also growl or purr while sleeping.

We don't know what cats dream about. Maybe your cat has just caught a mouse in its dream or it's dreaming of being tenderly petted.

In case you're wondering, a cat's dream can last about six minutes.

Pedigreed Cat Club. If you are looking for a particular breed of cat, your best bet is to contact a cat club devoted to that breed (see Useful Addresses, page 124). The club will provide you with addresses of breeders, who will also advise you on all aspects of cat ownership after you buy an animal. With unusual cat breeds or coat colors, you may have to wait quite a long time for a young kitten.

Cat Show. Here you have an opportunity to gather a large amount of information. You may even find a kitten that is up for sale.

Considerations When You Buy

When you visit a breeder to pick out a kitten, keep the following in mind:

■ The mother cat and her young should live in the breeder's home; they should not be housed in a cage.

■ Watch to see whether the breeder has a loving attitude toward the cats or treats them impersonally.

■ Before buying, check the animal's pedigree and look to see what organization issued it. Later on, you may want to take the animal to a cat show; it will

cost time and money if the pedigree of an unrecognized organization has to be transferred. The pedigree contains the names and colors of the cat's forebears (at least four generations). Any prizes won by the parents also can be recorded (for recognized organizations, see Useful Addresses, page 124).

■ A reputable breeder will not let the kittens go to new homes until they have had all their shots and are at least twelve weeks old.

■ In any case, draw up a contract of sale (see page 28).

■ Don't enter into any special agreements, such as the following: letting the breeder have a kitten from the first litter as the purchase price; the right of repurchase; the right of return; free stud service (see Breeding Pedigreed Cats, page 84).

■ Ask the breeder to give you the vaccination record and the pedigree at the time of purchase.

Health Check

When selecting a kitten, don't let your heart do all the talking. You also need to determine the state of the animal's health.

33

1. Checking the coat: bare spots on the coat are signs of illness.

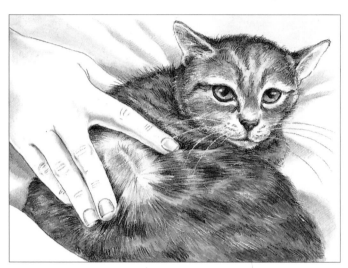

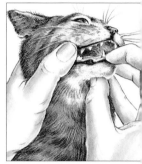

2. Red gums indicate some s... of infection.

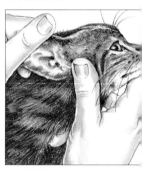

3. Watch for dirt when you check the ears.

4. Sex differences: A male ca... the right, a female on the lef...

Behavior. Healthy kittens romp boisterously and play with their litter mates adoringly. In between they take repeated nap breaks, often falling asleep immediately after a game has ended. With strangers they are usually reserved at first, but later their curiosity overcomes their caution.

Sick kittens, on the other hand, sit listlessly in a corner and seem downright apathetic.

Sex Determination. The sex of a kitten is easiest to determine shortly after it is born, since the genitals are not yet concealed by the coat at this time (see Drawing 4). Even later, though, it is relatively easy to determine the sex. The distance between the anus and the genital opening is greater in the male than in the female.

The genital opening of a male cat is distinctly round; in a female it is oval in shape.

Other Things to Look For. The anal area must be clean. Signs of caked-on feces in this area can be an indication of diarrhea (see Digestive Problems, page 77).

Examine the teeth and gums. The gums should be pale in color (see page 77).

In addition, check the ears for signs of infection or mites (see page 74).

A healthy kitten's eyes are bright, shiny, and clear.

How a Healthy Kitten Looks

Abdomen	Carefully palpate the kitten's abdomen. It should not seem excessively fat and bloated, since this can indicate a worm infestation. Keep in mind that a young kitten can consume an inordinate amount of food; right after eating its little belly is likely to seem quite plump and round.
Body	A young cat's body should be well padded and not too lean. In an older cat that is not pregnant, overweight can be recognized primarily by a sagging "potbelly." The normal weight of slender-bodied purebred cats is about 5½ pounds (2.5 kg); large-framed, well-developed domestic cats can weigh up to 12 pounds (5.5 kg).
Coat	The coat is clean. In young kittens it is soft to the touch; in older cats it is smooth and not shaggy. The coat should have a sheen. Bare spots are symptoms of disease.
Ears	The ears react to all sounds. Inside they are clean. Frequent shaking of the head and scratching at the ears are indications of an inflammation in the inner ear or of a mite infestation (see page 74).
Eyes	The eyes are clear and bright. Eyes that are reddened, shut, or smeared with mucus are signs of illness.
Nose	The nose is dry and warm, but not hot. The nostrils are free of mucus. The animal does not sneeze constantly and doesn't have a runny nose.
Teeth and Gums	The teeth of young kittens are not yet fully formed. With older cats, you need to make sure that no brownish-gray deposits (tartar) are visible on the teeth (see page 77). The gums should be pale in color. Reddened gums are signs of gingivitis.

The Most Popular Purebred Cats

The cat breeds described this section rank at the t of cat owners' popularity lis

Classification of the Breeds

The first deliberate attempts change the original form of domestic cat and to breed ot strains weren't made in t country until the end of century. How the ideal rep sentative of a certain breed supposed to look was spel out in detail, along with features and characterist that were desirable or unde able, in the breed standard.

Today, pedigreed cats divided into four large grou
■ Persian cats and exotic ca
■ medium-long-haired cats
■ short-haired cats, and
■ Siamese and Orien short-haired cats.

Coat Colors and Pattern

A wide variety of colors a coat patterns appear in bo domestic cats and pureb cats. I've divided them i seven large groups whose col

A British Shorthair. Its gray coat is called "blue."

and patterns are to be found in most domestic cats as well.

Within each cat breed there are different color varieties. For example, we currently distinguish among over 200 different colors and patterns with Persians.

Unicolored Cats. These cats can be black, white, blue, brown, chocolate, lilac, red, and cream.

Bicolored Cats. These animals have a more or less extensive share of white in their colored coat. There are also almost completely white cats with small colored areas (Turkish Van) and dark cats with small white marks (a blaze on the face, a white bib, or white socks). Tortoiseshell and blue-cream cats are common among all domestic

and purebred cats. These animals are always female, since the color red is always sex-linked in cats. With blue-cream cats, the blue and the cream should be well intermingled, not seen in the form of spots in the coat.

Tricolored Cats. These cats are always female. The tortoiseshell or blue-cream coloration is combined with white streaking or spotting. The combination of a gray or tawny striped coat with tortoiseshell is called Tortie-Tabby.

Cats with Points. They have a light-colored coat with dark areas on the head, tail, and feet (Siamese, Balinese); in Persians, this color variety is known as a Himalayan (color point).

Cats with Points and White Patches. The Siamese coloring is combined with unusual white patches that appear only on the four feet as gloves/mittens or socks (Birman). Siamese coloring with irregular white patches is the ragdoll.

Cats with "Tipping". In these cats, the hair tips are colored. The best-known type is black tipping (Chinchilla, Silver-shaded, and Smoke varieties). As purebreds, cats with tipping

Young kittens practice catching their prey with a toy mouse.

37

A wild-colored Abyssinian in its typical elegant appearance

occur also in blue, red, and tortoiseshell.

Striped Cats—"Tabbies." The coat exhibits a barred, blotched, ticked, or spotted pattern, usually in gray or brown. It occurs among wild cats, domestic cats, and pedigreed cats.

Abyssinian

The Abyssinian is one of the oldest breeds. A standard that specified the way it should look existed as early as the nineteenth century.

Appearance. Abyssinians have a medium-long, elegant, muscular body; their heads are more delicate and longer than that of the domestic cat. Abyssinians make a vivacious, athletic impression.

Coat. Their coats are short, soft, and thick. Each individual hair is banded; this phenomenon is known as Abyssinian ticking. Abyssinians are

A six-month-old Abyssinian kitten.

38

young British Shorthair. Only fter six weeks do the eyes cquire their typical color from old-orange to copper colored he adult cat, see p. 36).

often called "rabbit cats" because their fur resembles that of wild rabbits.

Color. The colors of the Abyssinian can be "wild" colors (warm brown/orange, black ticking); sorrel (coppery red, red-brown ticking), blue (blue-gray, steel-blue ticking), beige-fawn (matte beige, dark cream ticking), or silver (silver-white undercoat, ticking in appropriate color).

Eyes. The color of Abyssinians' eyes range from green through golden.

British Shorthair Blue (Chartreuse)

The genuine Chartreuse comes from France. The blue variety of the British Shorthair comes from England and is descended from English domestic cats mated with Persians.

Appearance. The Chartreuse has a large body with a muscular chest. The legs are short and sturdy, with round, strong feet. The head is round, with broad cheeks and a prominent chin.

Coat. The short, dense, fine coat with its dense undercoat stands out from the body like plush.

Color. They are light gray without shading. Gray that is based on uniform pigmentation of the hairs is called blue among breeders.

Eyes. Their eyes are bright yellow-orange through copper.

The Holy Birman

According to a legend of far-off Indochina, the Birman cats are descendants of the goddess of the transmigration of souls, Tsun-Kyan-Kse. More credible, however, is the assumption that Birmans originated around 1919, from a cross between Siamese and Persians. In 1963 it came to Germany from France.

Appearance. Its build is neither slender nor compact; rather, it is muscular and powerful, but elegant as well.

Coat. The coat is long, thick, and silken in texture, but the undercoat does not tangle or mat.

A lovely Birman cat, the blue point. It has blue-gray markings on the face, ears, paws, and tail.

A chocolate-colored Burmese cat. The short-haired coat is snug and very fine.

Color. The Holy Birman has a light beige body. Its face, tail, and legs are darker in color (like the Siamese).

Birmans are bred in many different colors. The best-known is the seal point with brown markings and the blue point with blue-gray markings. The pure white feet, or "gloves," end on the tips of the feet or the joint.

Eyes. The eyes are almost round and are a fascinating deep blue, a sign of partial albinism.

Burmese

Allegedly this cat originally came from monasteries in Burma, where it was cared for and revered by the monks. In 1930 an American brought a female specimen of these cats into the United States. The animal was mated with a Siamese, and that was the beginning of the first breeding program. Along with the Siamese, the Burmese continues to be one of the most popular short-haired breeds in America. The crossing of a Siamese and a Burmese is called the Tonkanese.

Appearance. Its body is medium in size and more powerful than the cat's appearance suggests. The body is blunt, wedge-shaped to a rounded head, which has a broad jaw and strong chin. In profile, the nose reveals a definite break.

The ears are set far apart on the head. They are broad at the base, with rounded tips.

Coat. The coat is short with glossy, thick, smooth, very fine hair, which lies close to the body.

Color. The original Burmese color is a rich, warm brown, which in terms of its genetic constitution is black. Today

41

A three-year-old Maine Coon cat, the blue-silver-tabby. It lies stretched out in the grass, relaxed, and yawns.

the Burmese also is bred in these colors: blue, chocolate, lilac, red, cream, tortoiseshell, blue-cream, chocolate tortie, seal tortie, blue tortie, and lilac tortie (see Tricolored Cats, page 37).

In all Burmese, the abdomen has to be somewhat lighter in color than the back and legs.

Eyes. The eyes are large and very expressive; their color is an amber-hued golden yellow and should be clear and bright.

Maine Coon

The Maine Coon is not a breed developed by man. It comes from North America, from the state of Maine, where it lives in the wild. As early as 100 years ago, it was held in high esteem as a mouser. For some years now, Maine Coons have been bred as a recognized breed throughout the world.

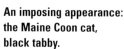

An imposing appearance: the Maine Coon cat, black tabby.

Norwegian Forest cat, black tabby with white. Its water-repelling coat protects it well from rain and snow.

Appearance. The Maine Coon is massive, muscular, and powerful; it's one of the biggest cat breeds. Males can reach a weight of 22 pounds (10 kg).

Coat. The coat is medium long and soft, with a thick undercoat and a bushy tail.

Color. All colors are allowed, except partial albinos (Siamese coloring).

Eyes. The eyes are green or golden orange; white cats have eyes of different colors (odd-eyed).

Norwegian Forest Cat

It developed in the damp, cold climate of Norway, probably through natural selection. Especially beautiful specimens were captured and used for breeding purposes. The Norwegian has been a recognized breed since 1975.

Appearance. The powerful, supple body seems taller in back than in front. The head is triangular with a long, straight nose and a strong chin. Lynxlike bunches of hair grow around the ears.

Coat. The coat is woolly underneath and covered with an outer coat of long, glossy hair. The full ruff is impressive.

Color. The color conforms to that of domestic cats. We recognize seven different color groups, including tabby, tabby with white, self-colored, and self-colored with white.

Eyes. The eye color matches the coat.

Persian

The Persian cat was previously known as the Angora. It originated in Asia Minor, where it was bred primarily in the color white and was a favorite plaything of ladies of the harem.

Appearance. The Persian has a powerful body on short, thick, heavily boned legs. The feet are large, round, and firm, with five toes on the front paws and four on the back paws. All the toes are very close together and covered by long tufts of hair. The tail is short and bushy, and has no kinks or knots.

The head of the Persian cat is round and massive, with a broad skull and tiny, round face. It sits atop a short, thick neck. The small, round, forward-tipped ears with their tufts of long hair are set low on the head and placed far apart. The

nose is short, blunt, and broad. The stop, or indentation, between the forehead and the nose is typical of the profile of the Persian cat. Full cheeks, a strong, well-developed chin, and a wide, powerful jaw are also typical of the Persian.

Coat. The coat is long, thick, glossy, fine-textured, and uniform in length.

Still a bit awkward, the baby kitten makes its first climbing attempts.

A color point Persian. Left: Seal point; right: Creme point.

...mese are masters at ...mbing. No tree is too ...h for them.

A Siamese with typical markings.

Color. Currently there are more than 200 different colors.

Eyes. The large round eyes of the Persian are mostly copper-colored or dark orange. The eyes are blue or odd-eyed with a white coat; and green with Silver-Tabby, Golden, and Chinchilla; and blue with Himalayan/color point.

Siamese

According to legend, the Siamese was kept as a temple cat in Siam, now known as Thailand. By the end of the nineteenth century this cat was very popular and a breed standard was established.

Appearance. The Siamese has an elegant, slender, fine-limbed body and moves with extreme grace. The cat has a wedge-shaped head with long, straight nose and large, deep-set, pointed ears.

Coat. The coat is thick, very short, glossy, and conforms to the body.

Color. This cat's special feature is its unusual markings (points). The body is a uniform color; "pointed" with another color. There are many different color variations.

Eyes. The eyes are brilliant blue, large, and slanted.

Distinctive Characteristics. Slightly crossed eyes were once the mark of the true Siamese. Today this is considered a defect.

The kink in the tail is also considered a defect. Animals that possess it are excluded from breeding.

45

Proper Care
and Grooming

By looking at your cat, you can tell whether
it is happy in your household: bright eyes;
a glossy, velvety-soft coat; and an athletic
body. Its lively behavior speaks for itself:
"I like it here."

A thorough cat washing. A cat
cleans itself from top to bottom
many times a day.

What Kitty Needs

If your cat is going to li
indoors with you, you shou
acquire a few items in order
provide for your pet's needs.

Litter Box

Plastic Pans or Trays. Wi
a protective rim that tu
inward, these pans are practi
since almost no litter can
pawed out.

*Enclosed Litter Boxes with
Roof.* This type of box has t
advantage of keeping the stro
urine odor from penetrati
into your entire house. The t
should be about 16 inches (
cm) high.

Automatic Toilets. After t
cat has used the toilet, t
litter is carried away on a ki
of conveyor belt and fre
litter is added. Another mo
neutralizes the odor by mea
of electrical current.

Preparing and Cleaning
Litter Box. Fill the litter b
with litter to a depth of abo
2–3 inches (5–8 cm). It i
good idea to get a spec
sieve-shovel (available

**Cats love a warm cuddly pla
to rest. A soft pillow can als
invite one for a nap.**

atched over by mom, the kitten
n slumber wonderfully. Mom takes
re of the coat at the same time.

pet stores) to remove the
excrement, because it allows
unused litter to fall back into
the box.

Removing the excrement is
extremely important—cats
will not use an unclean litter
box. Instead, they will find a
little corner of your house or
apartment to use as a toilet.

The cat's box needs to
be emptied completely and
washed out with hot water
once a week.

Food and Water Bowls

Food and Water Dishes. Dishes
made of ceramics or porcelain
are sturdy, dishwasher-proof,
and safe for use in the micro-
wave. A bowl with a diameter
of about 8 inches (20 cm) is
adequate for moist food or for
water. For dry food you can use
a higher, smaller bowl (about 4
inches, or 10 cm, across).

Food Dispensers. Dispensers
for dry food are available in
pet stores. Automatic food

dispensers with a timer switch can come in handy when you want to go away for the weekend and are unable to locate a cat sitter.

Cleaning Food and Water Dishes. They have to be cleaned every day with hot water.

Travel Carriers

Carrying Cases Made of Plastic. These carriers are easy to clean and to disinfect. Cases that have a latching iron-mesh door can be disassembled to save space.

Special Plastic Carrying Bags. One side of the carrying bag has a transparent plastic window, while the other is provided with air holes, and a zipper to close the case. This type of bag is suitable and safe for cats.

Wicker Baskets. Baskets that are equipped with a wire-mesh door look very attractive. However, the cat could be injured by a sharp piece of willow protruding from the basketweave.

Scratching Post

Cats need to sharpen their claws, which are important tools needed in fighting with rivals, catching prey, and climbing.

Outdoor cats sharpen their claws on tree trunks. Indoor cats have to be given an opportunity to sharpen them without harming your upholstered furniture or wallpaper.

For sharpening claws, pet stores offer scratching boards that can be mounted on the wall at a slight angle. Disposable cardboard scratching boards are also suitable for this purpose, as are upright posts, angled posts or "trees" for scratching and climbing, and floor-to-ceiling models in

A flap for coming and going.

A kitty potty with lid.

A "kennel" for transporting.

Toys of every sort for the well-developed need to play.

50

A cat needs a scratching post with sitting platforms and holes to feel comfortable. From there it can enjoy the view.

which the cat can climb into snugly "caves."

Fasten the equipment to the floor or mount it on the wall or ceiling with angle bars; no cat will use a wobbly scratching tree a second time. I "created" my own scratching equipment/ toy for my cats, using buckets that once held laundry detergent. Thoroughly wash the containers and glue carpeting to the outside.

A Place to Sleep

Pet stores can provide round, cozy "igloos" or "caves," baskets with a soft cushion, a real cat sofa, and much more as places for your cat to sleep.

You also can cover a normal cardboard box (16 × 16 × 16 inches, or 40 × 40 × 40 cm) with carpeting.

Toys

Most of all cats like to play with a living creature. That can be a mouse, another cat, or the cat's owner. But toys also provide stimuli.

Commercial cat toys are usually designed to appeal to the cat's hunting instinct. Homemade toys, however, are easy to create (see Great Ideas for Playing With Your Cat, page 106).

The Cat's Realm: A Happy Home

Your home, balcony, and yard can be made into a real cat paradise if you make a few allowances for "feline taste" when you decorate.

Your Home: The Cat's Domain

If you know your velvet-pawed housemate's likes and dislikes, even a one-room apartment can be made into an interesting realm for your cat. You need to remember that

■ cats do a round of their "territory" several times a day (The more variety each round offers, the better.);

■ cats hate closed doors inside the house;

■ cats appreciate having several cozy places to rest in their home;

■ cats like to climb and balance;

■ cats prefer to observe things "from on high";

■ cats are fond of hiding places and all sorts of nooks and crannies;

■ cats like to perch by the window, since they love watching what is going on outdoors; sitting by the window also allows cats to absorb the warmth of the sun.

Cats love to balance on fences and railings. It is therefore recommended that you safety proof your balcony and garden.

52

Why Do Cats Sleep So Much?

A day has twenty-four hours, and your cat will sleep for some sixteen of them. It doesn't really rest more than a person in a single span, but instead spreads out its "naps" over the entire day.

A cat needs so much sleep because of its eating pattern. Hunting mice can take quite a bit of energy and can make a cat sleepy. The same holds true for domestic cats who "catch" only their toy mice.

Eliminating Potential Hazards

Indoors. Never leave any sharp objects such as sewing and knitting needles or shards lying around. The cat could swallow these small objects. A cat can get tangled up in threads and balls of wool. Cats can burn themselves on hot stove burners, irons that have not been turned off, burning candles, and open, unprotected fires in a fireplace. Erasers, rubber rings, plastic toys, and silver tinsel cannot be digested by cats and can lead to serious health problems.

Cats like to creep into "caves" such as open washing machines, drawers, and plastic bags left lying around, but there is a danger of suffocation. Wall sockets need to be secured, to keep the cat from getting a jolt of electrical current. Detergents and cleansers, as well as chemicals, can poison a cat or cause an acid burn. Never leave cigarettes lying around. If your cat eats a cigarette, the nicotine it contains can produce symptoms of poisoning (see page 81). Use only nonpoisonous house plants (see page 56). Make sure windows are secured.

Outdoors. Make balconies secure so that the cat cannot fall off (see page 56). You can even enclose your yard with an electric fence (see page 56). Store antifreeze, fuel oil, motor oil, and pesticides where the cat cannot get at them. Such substances could cause severe poisoning (see page 81).

Making the Windows and Balcony Safe

Windows. Not only can a cat get out through an open window and run away, but it can also fall to its death. Even windows left partially open or tilted have cost more than one cat its life. When trying to climb out, a cat can get caught in the opening and be unable to get free again. Using a screen or a somewhat sturdier homemade window safety device will enable you to leave the window open without worrying and protect the cat at the same time. For a homemade safeguard, fit a wooden frame into the open window, attach spot-welded screen wire, and fasten it to the window frame with bolts. This allows your cat to enjoy the fresh air and remain safe at the same time.

A Cat-friendly Apartment

It doesn't take much at all to provide your cat with what it needs to feel comfortable. You just have to remember the cat's preferences. It is important that all the doors (except the front door of the apartment) be left open for the cat so that it has unimpeded access to every room.

A Little Cat Paradise

Balcony. Cats appreciate a balcony because it is a vantage point and an observation point that offers a great deal of variety. A net will keep the cat from falling off ①. The balcony's protective railing has been extended with a board ②, so the cat has room to lie down comfortably.

Living Area. Cats wander through their territory several times a day. This "cat path" ③ made of shelves and cleverly arranged cupboards makes the cat's daily round into an adventure. Next to the extended window ledge, which serves as a lookout ④, there is cat grass ⑤ to nibble (see page 62).

The padded pillow ⑥ near the radiator provides a place to sleep. A special loungin hammock, which is attache to another radiator, offe another wonderful place rest ⑦.

Toys ⑧ are a must to ke the cat from getting bored.

Small bucket or pail ⑨ c also be tumbled about for fu

This is how a living space set up for your cat's needs could look.

he scratching tree ⑩ discourages the cat from sharpening its claws on the furniture. This model, equipped with platforms, also tempts the kitty to climb and do gymnastics. If you have no room for large scratching posts, you can mount a space-saving scratching board on the wall ⑪.

In addition, the cats needs its own spot for feeding bowls and the litter box.

Kitchen. The food and water dishes are placed on a vinyl placemat. Cats like to drag their food out of the bowl. A placemat will keep you from having to clean the floor.

Bathroom. The litter box is located in the bathroom. It should stand in a quiet corner out of the way. The bathroom floor is usually tiled and easy to clean.

Balcony. Not infrequently cats fall to their death. There are nets that can be secured with guy ropes (available in pet stores).

Making the Yard Safe

There is a possibility that a cat allowed out in the yard will run away; moreover, a strange dog might also get into the yard and chase your pet. For these reasons it is critical to make it possible for your cat to have access to the house or apartment at any time.

Cat Door. A cat door will allow the cat to go in and out of your apartment or house unhindered (see photo, page 50). You can install the door in your front or street door, terrace door, or cellar door. Pet stores carry cat doors in a variety of designs. You can install them yourself or have a professional do the job.

There is a special type of cat door available that can keep out strange cats. It will open only if the cat is wearing the appropriate "magnetic key" on its collar.

Fences. Often an outer fence that curves inward is sufficient to keep the kitty from climbing over and to secure your garden. Tall trees

Beware of the Plants

Cats like to chew on green, growing things. If a cat has no special cat grass available, it may resort to "swiping" a few bites of plants that it cannot digest. It can even poison itself in the process.

POISONOUS to Cats

Adonis, anemone, autumnal crocus, azalea ● belladonna, birthwort, box wood, black nightshade, bracken, broom ● calla, castor oil plant, Chinese primrose, Christ's-thorn, common celandine, coral tree ● daffodil, daphne, datura, delphinium, dieffenbachia, dwarf elder ● equisetum (horsetail), ● fir trees, foxglove, fool's parsley ● globeflower, green lily ● (spotted) hemlock, hepatica, hyacinth ● ivy ● laburnum, lily of the valley, lupine ● male fern, miracle shrub, mistletoe, monkshood ● oleander ● philodendron, poinsettia, potato vine, pulsatilla (meadow pasqueflower) ● ranunculus, robinia (locust tree) ● scarlet runner, snowdrop, spindle tree, spruce ● tobacco plant, tomato plant ● veilweed ● wartweed (euphorbia), white hellebore

NOT HARMFUL to Cats

If you want do both your cat and yourself a favor, you can plant the following in tubs, balcony planter boxes, or garden beds (see page 62): catnip ● cypress grass ● feverfew ● field mint ● gold balm evening primrose ● lemon balm ● true thyme ● valerian ● water mint ● wild thyme

56

the open window has been secured with a net or screen, our cat can sit safely on the windowsill.

can be provided with screen wire collars to prevent the cat from climbing up.

Cat lovers with technical expertise can surround their yard with an electric fence. When the cat touches the fence, it will receive a mild electric shock that will discourage it from trying to get out of the yard at that spot again. The cat will not be injured.

Usually the electric fence can be "deactivated" again after a few weeks, since cats quickly learn not to repeat bad experiences.

Good Nutrition Is Critical

Fresh mouse would certainly sell like hotcakes if it appeared on a menu designed for cats. But even without this dish, a declared favorite of felines, you can provide your pet with a well-balanced diet.

Commercial Cat Food Keeps a Cat Fit

No cat owner is in a position to feed his or pet freshly killed prey. Apart from that, the danger of transmitting germs and parasites, with which prey is often infected, would be very great (see page 76).

However, it is easy to feed your pet a nutritious, well-balanced diet. The commercial foods available for cats provide complete nutrition in a great variety of forms and different flavors, including beef, poultry, fish, and lamb.

Canned Cat Food. This type of food contains everything a cat needs to stay healthy: protein, fat, carbohydrates, vitamins, minerals, and trace elements. To a great extent it conforms to the nutritional components found in prey. It is ready to use at any time, has a long shelf life, and can be served quickly. A wide range of canned food varieties from different manufacturers is available on the market. You can compare the ingredients of these products by reading the information on the label. Canned food consists of a mixture of meat, cereal, vegetables, and yeast.

Dry Cat Food. This type of food is also nutritionally complete and is available in various flavors and in different sizes of kibble. Dry food differs from canned food in its moisture composition (canned food is 75 percent water; dry food contains only 15 percent). For this reason, it is especially important always to provide a cat with fresh water in addition to dry food, so that it can get all the liquid it requires. Dry food is more concentrated and thus higher in energy than canned food, so your pet's servings can be reduced somewhat. Follow the guidelines suggested on the package.

Special Diets

In some cases it is a good idea to put your cat on a special diet. Let a veterinarian make the decision. There are excellent commercial diet foods available for cats, designed especially for pets who are overweight or suffer

When cats drink, they form
their long tongue into a spoon
and scoop the liquid into their
mouth.

Tips on Feeding

After meals	The cat wants to be left in peace; don't play with it now.
Bones	Dangerous, especially poultry bones. They can get stuck in the cat's throat.
Dog food	Too low in protein; use only once in a while, if necessary.
Feeding time	At the same time every day, ideally in the morning and again in the evening
Food amounts	Canned food: Young cats, about 3.2 ounces (90 g); adult cats, about 7–12 ounces (200–350 g); lactating cats, about 16 ounces (450 g) daily.
Food and water dishes	Wash in hot water daily.
Food quality	Compare the ingredients listed on the product labels.
Food temperature	Serve food at room temperature, never straight from the refrigerator.
Meat	Use only cooked meat and do not feed meat exclusively.
Mouse catchers	Even cats that have an opportunity to catch mice need to be fed regularly.
Number of feedings	Small kittens 3–4 times a day, adult cats 1–2 times a day, old cats 3 times a day, pregnant cats 1–2 times a day, lactating cats 3–4 times a day.
Pureed food	Recommended for older sick cats only.
Switching to a different food	Cats are creatures of habit; it's very difficult to switch to another food. If you use high-quality commercial cat food, there is no need for a change.
Uneaten food	Remove immediately to prevent germs.
Where to feed	Always in the same undisturbed place, in peace and quiet.

from kidney diseases, metabolic disorders, allergies, or chronic diarrhea. High-protein diets of excellent nutritive value can be used for getting a cat back on its feet again after a serious illness. Commercial diet formulas are sold in the form of dry or canned food, and they are available from veterinarians.

The following diet has proved successful for cats suffering from mild gastro-intestinal upsets (diarrhea, constipation).

Diet for Gastrointestinal Problems. First, don't feed the cat for one to two days; then feed it as follows for the next three to five days.

Recipe: Mix two parts cottage cheese with one part mashed potatoes (prepared with water).

Over the course of the day serve the cat five small portions, each one prepared freshly (about one heaping tablespoonful in a serving). After two or three days, you can replace the cottage cheese with boiled lamb, beef, veal, poultry, or fish.

Because animals lose lots of liquids with diarrhea, the cat always needs to have fresh drinking water available to

which you can add a pinch of salt.

Food Allergies

Commercial cat food ingredients can trigger allergies in some cats (see page 58). Frequently only the veterinarian can determine the correlations between the diet and the allergic reaction. Special diets help, both in obtaining a diagnosis and in treating the allergy.

The Right Drink

Water. This is the best drink for cats. The water bowl must be cleaned and filled with fresh water daily. Put the bowl in a place that is accessible to your pet at all times. Some cats prefer stale water from flower vases, puddles, or aquariums. As long as the cat always has fresh water in its bowl, this is nothing to worry about. Some cats like to drink directly from an open faucet; others even drink water from the toilet bowl.

Milk. This contains plenty of protein and calcium; it is a valuable food, especially for lactating cats. You should use whole milk, not low-fat milk. Never thin it with water. Cat's milk is somewhat higher in fat

you have several cats living with you, each one should have its own food bowl to avoid any conflicts.

and protein than cow's milk. You may dilute condensed milk with water.

There are many cats that like to drink milk and tolerate it well, but milk causes diarrhea in some cats. The sugar—lactose—not the fat brings on the laxative effect. When milk sours, the lactose is broken down. That is why curdled milk, yogurt, and curd cheese do not act as laxatives.

Cat Grass

Cats love to nibble on something green. We do not know exactly why, but we do know that it probably aids their digestion in some way. Long-haired cats, in particular, swallow a great many hairs when they groom their coats with their tongues. By consuming plant parts, they are able to bring up "hairballs" that have collected in their stomach.

Cats are especially fond of cypress grass, but ordinary grass, oats, wheat, and cat grass, which pet stores sell already sowed in boxes, are popular as well.

Homemade Meals

What cat owner wouldn't love to spoil his or her pet with a

A cat waits intently before a mouse hole.

If the mouse dares to leave the cat grabs at it.

e mouse might not be killed
mediately with a single bite
the nape. The cat often plays
vhile with its prey.

tasty, home-prepared meal occasionally? I too cook for my cats on occasion. However, I urge you not to cook all your pet's meals yourself, because it is not easy to prepare a nutritionally balanced diet. It is absolutely essential to ensure that certain nutritional elements are present in the food. The cat's digestive system is able to offset too small or too large a supply of essential nutrients over a short period of time.

Over the long run, however, serious damage can occur if the cat is fed improperly. Health problems will result if the cat has an inadequate supply of the following most important

nutrients: vitamin B_1 (thiamin), vitamin E, vitamin A, taurine, arachidonic acid, and calcium.

Over an extended period of time, an oversupply of certain vital nutrients such as vitamin A, vitamin D, and calcium will also lead to pathological disorders.

Special Meals

I have designed the following cat dinners so that they contain everything essential for good nutrition. My cats thoroughly relish these dishes. Please keep in mind, however, that you can spoil a cat very quickly. After an especially tasty meal, your pet may be unwilling to eat anything else. These treats should be offered only on rare occasions.

Each recipe is the equivalent of one day's rations for an adult cat who is not nursing kittens.

Christmas Dinner

7 ounces (200 g) carp
1/4 cup boiled rice
1 teaspoon butter
Pinch of salt

Steam the fish in a little water for twenty minutes. Add the boiled rice, stir in the

butter, and season with salt to taste.

Easter Dinner

3.5 ounces (100 g) of lamb
1 tablespoon oil
Pinch of herbes de Provence
8 ounces (1/4 liter) meat broth

Cut the lamb into small pieces and brown it in oil. Stir in the herbes de Provence and broth. Let simmer for thirty minutes. Serve with mashed potatoes, prepared with water.

Roasted Fowl

1 chicken breast
1 teaspoon butter
1 pinch of vitamin paste (available in pet stores)

Braise the chicken in butter for about thirty minutes. Remove it from the pan and

Why Do Cats Catch Mice?

Cats have already been living a long time with humans. Even so they have remained predators like their relatives, the big cats, which include the lion, the tiger, and the leopard. The animals of prey for cats are much smaller. Most of all cats love mice. The hunting instinct is inborn. Even when you regularly feed your cat, it will not pass up an opportunity to chase after any mouse that crosses its path.

Cats have great persistence in hunting. They can sit quietly for hours in front of a mouse hole. If a mouse finally does stick its little head out, the cat will first wait patiently. The mouse shouldn't be immediately afraid and disappear again into its hole. If the mouse dares to come out a little further, the cat will spring as quickly as lightning and catch the mouse.

What should you do if your cat drags you a mouse? While it might seem disgusting to you, for the cat it is a great part of life. So don't scold your cat. Take the mouse away as soon as the cat has left it and put it outside. If the mouse is dead, you can bury it.

e cat moistens its paws
th its tongue to wash its
ce with them.

t: After each meal the cat
ks its face thoroughly.

spread the vitamin paste on it.
Cut the meat into small pieces.

Luzi's Kidney Goulash
1/2 a beef kidney
1 tablespoon noodles, boiled
1 teaspoon flaked yeast

Soak the beef kidney in
milk for three to four hours.
Cook about ten minutes in a
pressure cooker, then cut into
pieces. Add the boiled noodles
and sprinkle the yeast flakes
over the top.

Grooming Is Not Just Beautifying

Good care also includ[es] thorough grooming ro[u]tines for your cat. You ca[n] sometimes detect early war[n]ing signs of illness.

Grooming Aids

Short-haired Cats. Use a fin[e] toothed metal comb, a bru[sh] with natural bristles, a spon[ge] with rubber nubs, and [a] chamois cloth for short-haire[d] cats.

Long-haired Cats. Use [a] sturdy metal comb with coar[se] and fine teeth, a brush wi[th] natural bristles, a comb with handle, and a ripping comb [to] remove knots in the coats [of] long-haired cats.

Coat Care

You need to comb out t[he] loose hairs of short-haired ca[t] only during molting season.

Cats with medium-leng[th] hair and especially Persia[ns] must be thoroughly comb[ed] and brushed daily. The hairs [it] swallows will form hairballs [in] its stomach, which are no[r]mally vomited up. Par[ti]cularly with Persians, ho[w]

Natural claw care: The Persi[an] cat sharpens its claws on a tree trunk.

he tongue with its rough apillae is an excellent tool r cleaning.

ever, hairballs can cause constipation or even lead to intestinal blockage.

Combing and Brushing

Long-haired Cats. Put the cat on your lap. Starting with the coarse-toothed metal comb, comb the cat's abdomen in the direction that the coat lies. The cat's undercoat is especially fine in these places, and it can form mats quickly. Then,

with the fine-toothed metal comb, go over the entire coat again, from head to tail. Be on the lookout for parasites (see page 72) and check the skin. After combing, brush thoroughly.

Short-haired Cats. First comb the coat with the fine-toothed metal comb; then, go over the coat with the lightly dampened sponge with rubber nubs. Finally, give it a rubdown

Health Check During Routine Grooming

	Healthy Cat	Sick Cat
Anus	Clean	Smeared with feces
Behavior	Alert, frisky, affectionate	Apathetic and indifferent
Breathing	Quiet, even	Panting, puffing
Coat	Glossy, clean	Dull, oily, smeary, tufted, infested with parasites (see page 72)
Ears	Completely clean	Smeary secretions (see page 74); reddened inflammation
Eyes	Clear, bright, open	Tearing, stuck shut, discharge
Feces	Moist, soft, dark gray	Pasty or liquid, bloody to brown
Gums	Good pink color	Pale, blood-red
Nose	Dry or cool	Wet, whitish or yellowish discharge
Skin	Dry, smooth	Scaly, oily, red spots
Teeth	Whitish, not coated	Brown-gray tartar (see page 77)

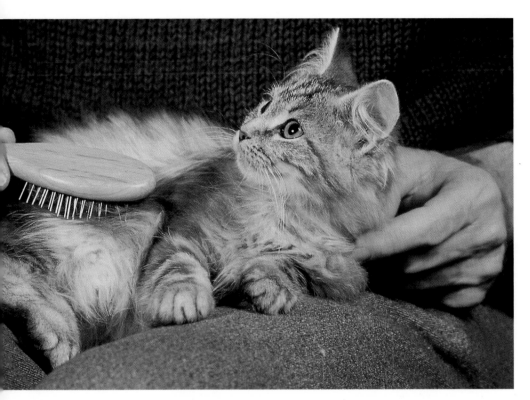

**ong-haired cats must be
made comfortable with regular
combing and brushing from
the very beginning.**

along the lie of the coat with a damp chamois cloth.

Untangling Knots

Long-haired cats often develop little knots of hair. To undo them, separate the knot into small sections with your fingers and try to untangle the knot with a comb that has a handle. You may have to cut through the knot with a small ripping tool (from a sewing supplies store) or with a dematting comb (from a pet store).

Bathing

A cat needs to be bathed only when its coat is extremely dirty, the veterinarian instructs you to bathe it, or one to two days before it is going to appear in a cat show. Overly frequent bathing is harmful to the skin. You can learn how to best bathe your cat on page 71.

69

The Well-groomed Cat

By nature a cat is very clean. Several times a day it washes its coat thoroughly with its tongue. Accordingly, the colloquial expression "to have a cat lick" in the sense of "to have a superficial wash" is completely unjustified. Nevertheless, from time to time you will need to supplement your cat's grooming.

Cleaning the Eyes

Normally a cat's eyes are clear and clean. Slight encrustations may be removed with a soft, dampened paper tissue (see Drawing 1). Always wipe carefully, going from the ear toward the nose.

Signs of Illness. Heavy tearing that appears suddenly can indicate the presence of a foreign body in the eye.

Some Persians suffer from constant tearing, caused by the short nose produced by breeding. Frequently related to that is a narrowing or congestion of the tear duct. All you can do is to dab the tears away with a paper tissue several times a day.

Ear Check

Cats' ears are normally clean. The external parts of the ear—particularly in outdoor cats—

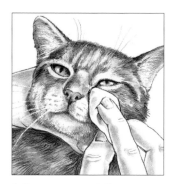

1. Remove encrustations around the eyes with a paper tissue.

may get rather dirty. If that happens, carefully wipe the ear with a damp paper tissue.

Signs of Illness. If the cat shakes its head frequently and keeps scratching at its ear, this may be an indication of mites whose feces can be recognized in the form of dark little clumps (see page 74). A variety of skin diseases produce this same behavior in a cat. It is essential to consult a veterinarian.

Tooth Check

You should occasionally check your cat's teeth (see drawing, page 34). Both domestic cats and purebreds have a tendency to develop tartar and gum inflammations (gingivitis).

2. Bathe the cat when it is ver

3. Clean the coat with a speci

4. Wipe the wet coat with a previously warmed towel.

5. Loosen hair knots carefully with your fingers.

Signs of Illness. Tartar is visible as a thick, brownish-gray coating on the teeth, and it often is accompanied by bad breath. If the tartar is not removed by a veterinarian, the gums can become inflamed.

Bathing

Your cat should be bathed only in exceptional cases (see page 69). Bathe your pet in the sink in warm water from 86 to 95°F (30–35°C) and use baby shampoo or a special moisturizing shampoo. Hold the cat's front feet firmly with one hand while you wash it with the other—keep its head dry! After the bath, wrap the cat in a heated towel and carefully rub it dry. Keep it in a warm room until its coat is dry.

Checking the Anal Region

Accumulations of feces around the anus are a sign of diarrhea. Clean the anus and the surrounding area with a damp cloth. Persistent diarrhea is a warning sign of many dangerous diseases. Seek the advice of a veterinarian.

Claw Care

The claws of some indoor cats grow much too long. They have to be trimmed with special clippers (available in pet stores). When you cut them, try not to injure the quick, the part of the claw with blood vessels. Hold the claws against a strong light when you cut them. If you don't trust yourself to clip your pet's claws, have a veterinarian do it.

Preventive Care and Health Problems

L ike all other living creatures, cats are vulnerable to
disease. You can at least have
your pet vaccinated against
the most dangerous infectious diseases as a preventive
measure.

Protection for Man and Beast

Every cat, whether a domestic
cat or a purebred, needs to
be taken to a veterinarian
immediately after it joins your
household. Only he or she will
be able to assess the state of
your cat's health accurately,
check it for parasites, and
recommend any needed
inoculations.

Vaccinations. They offer the
best form of protection against
the most dangerous infectious
diseases of cats, including
feline distemper and feline
respiratory disease (see table,
page 79).

Immunity is guaranteed
only if the cat is vaccinated at
certain specified intervals (see
Vaccination Schedule, page
74).

Worming. This frees the cat
from potential intestinal parasites such as roundworms
(ascarids) and tapeworms (see
page 75). Because these parasites also can attack humans,

young kittens are wormed as a
preventive measure.

Worming

Young kittens are given their
first treatment at the age of
two weeks. The treatment is
repeated weekly until the
twelfth week of life.

Kittens over twelve weeks
old and adult cats are wormed
about every three months.

Breeding females are
wormed two weeks after they
give birth and then at fourteen
day intervals until the kittens
are weaned.

If the worm infestation
is severe, the cat has to
be wormed immediately. The
treatment will have to be
repeated after two to three
weeks.

External Parasites

In technical terms external
parasites are known as
ectoparasites, which settle on
the cat's skin or coat.

■ *Fleas:* Fleas and their
excrement are visible as black
dots when you comb through
the cat's coat.

Control. Very good flea-
control products (medicines
that can be taken orally, drops,
powders, or shampoos) are
available.

evention is better than
eatment. There are several
ings you can do to prevent
ur cat from becoming ill.

You need to disinfect the cat's surroundings as well, including its bed and blanket and the floor.

A flea collar can act as a preventive, dispensing an insecticide over a period of about three to four months. However, the cat will be constantly in contact with the toxin. In addition, outdoor cats have been known to die from strangulation because of a collar.

■ *Lice:* These light-yellow insects live on the cat's skin. They attack primarily ill-groomed and weakened animals, but they will not live on humans. They are visible to the naked eye.

Control. See Fleas, page 72. The surroundings do not have to be disinfected because lice live exclusively on their host's body.

■ *Ticks:* They burrow into the cat's skin to suck its blood. Ticks appear primarily in spring and late summer.

Control. Check the cat thoroughly for ticks every time it has been outdoors, especially during the warm seasons. Use tweezers to rotate ticks out of your pet's skin. Rotate the tweezers in any direction you choose. A tick collar can serve as a preventive.

■ *Ear Mites:* They attack the cat's inner ear and can be detected by the presence of a crumbly, crusty coating in the ear. The cat shakes its head constantly and scratches at its ear. The infestation is passed from one animal to another.

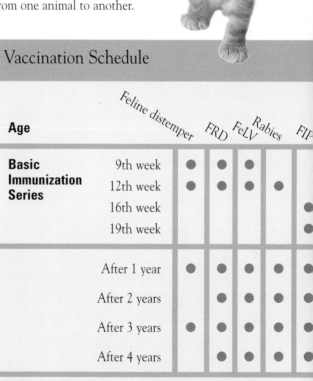

Vaccination Schedule

Age		Feline distemper	FRD	FeLV	Rabies	FIP
Basic Immunization Series	9th week	●	●	●		
	12th week	●	●	●	●	
	16th week					●
	19th week					●
	After 1 year	●	●	●	●	●
	After 2 years		●	●	●	●
	After 3 years	●	●	●	●	●
	After 4 years		●	●	●	●

Important: Vaccinations are not effective immediately. It takes one to two weeks for immunity to develop.

healthy happy quartet: Under
other's watchful care, the
tle kittens dare to venture
en to the nearest tree.

Control. The veterinarian will clean the auditory canals and administer a salve that kills mites.

Internal Parasites

The technical term for internal parasites is endoparasites. They infest the cat's intestine and other organs. Among the most common parasites are the roundworm (ascarid) and the tapeworm.

■ *Roundworms:* Adult cats become infected with this common worm species by ingesting the eggs of roundworms that are present on the ground or in their coat. Baby cats can become infected through their mother's milk. If the infestation is mild, worms that are excreted in the cat's stool will not be visible to the naked eye. If the infestation is severe, the cat could vomit up worms.

Control. The veterinarian will have suitable remedies on hand. Cats that are not wormed grow thin, and their coats lose luster. In young kittens, the overall process of physical development can be delayed. In rare cases, these worms also infest humans.

■ *Tapeworms:* The cat tapeworm is a very common worm

75.

species. It is transmitted when cats eat infected mice. Mice are carriers of tapeworm larvae. There is one tapeworm species that is transmitted by fleas as well. The tapeworm segments, which resemble grains of rice, are excreted by cats in their stool. Sometimes they can be seen in the stool or stuck to the hairs near the anus.

Control. Every worm infestation can be safely controlled by the veterinarian, without any danger to the cat.

Toxoplasmosis

The cat contracts toxoplasmosis from infected prey (mice) or by consuming infected raw meat. No contagion is possible if the cat never is given raw meat, has no contact with the excreta of other cats, and never gets the opportunity to catch a mouse.

In a cat, toxoplasmosis can proceed in the form of intestinal disease completely undetected. Almost all people who have frequent contact with animals or like to eat raw ground meat have already had toxoplasmosis.

If you are pregnant, as a precaution you should be tested for toxoplasmosis antibodies. If you are not immune,

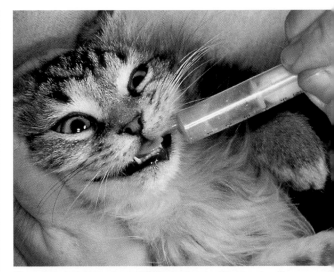

You can administer drops with a syringe without a needle.

The cat can also lick some medications from your finger.

76

be especially careful with personal hygiene when dealing with cats.

Diseases of the Mouth and Teeth

Tartar and gingivitis are quite common especially in elderly cats. The cause is often a liver or kidney disease.

Tartar. It can be seen as a thick, brownish-gray coating on the teeth. The veterinarian will anesthetize the cat and use ultrasound to remove the tartar.

Gingivitis. It is indicated by an extremely dark red coloration of the gums. Treatment is usually protracted.

Digestive Problems

Diarrhea. Young cats in particular are susceptible to digestive upsets, which frequently take the form of diarrhea. The animal's behavior meanwhile remains completely normal. Often the stool quickly will return to normal if you stop feeding the cat at once and give it an opportunity to drink plenty of fresh water (see page 61). If the diarrhea persists, it is imperative to consult a veterinarian.

Constipation. The cat tries to defecate but fails, despite strenuous bearing down. Elderly Persian cats become constipated quite frequently, possibly because of insufficient exercise.

Fresh liver or milk sometimes can help to remedy the situation. Gently massaging the cat's abdomen or giving it an enema (commercially available baby enemas) can bring relief. However, the cause has to be determined by a veterinarian.

Vomiting. Occasional vomiting, after eating plant parts, for example, is no cause for concern in cats. If the vomiting occurs with greater frequency, the animal should be taken to a veterinarian.

Diseases of the Eye and Nose

Conjunctivitis. Cats frequently develop conjunctivitis, or inflammation of the mucous membrane lining the inner surface of the eyelid and the exposed surface of the eyeball. The disorder can often be ascribed to the feline respiratory disease complex (see Infectious Diseases, page 79). Young kittens scarcely looked after on farms, for example, are especially at risk. The inflammation is often accompanied

by pus, caused by bacteria that attack the mucous membranes. The eyelids are swollen, and the rims of the lids and the eyelashes are so sticky that the animals no longer can open their eyes. Usually these cats go blind or die of exhaustion. Conjunctivitis requires lengthy treatment by the veterinarian, excellent care, and a highly nutritious diet.

Colds and Coughs. Colds and respiratory noises can be caused by accumulations of mucus in the air passages. These infections carry a danger of pneumonia, which is usually accompanied by fever and apathy and can prove fatal. Only the veterinarian can help your pet.

The Older Cat

The life expectancy of a cat that is lovingly taken care of and groomed can be fifteen years and more. Often, age-related problems appear only when cats reach a very advanced age. The cat does not clean itself as frequently as before; its eyesight and hearing may begin to fail; and the joints show signs of wear and tear. Dental problems give the cat trouble, and its appetite diminishes. Your pet needs your affection and understanding now more than ever.

Euthanasia. If your cat is no longer able to live free of pain, you need to ask your veterinarian to put it to sleep. Your cat will be given an injection that contains a narcotic substance. For someone who has lived with a pet for many years, seeing the cat's suffering and witnessing its death is a painful, sad experience. But in the final analysis, setting the animal free from its torment is the last proof of love a cat owner can offer. It goes without saying that you will stay at the cat's side until it has drawn its very last breath.

Why Do Cats Land Safely on Their Feet?

Cats can survive falls even from great heights. They land almost always on all fours. They can do this by using their tails as rudders. You can imagine it like this: as the cat falls, it uses its tail to help it turn its body around in the air so that its feet will be beneath it just before it hits the ground.

This way it ensures that it will land on all fours.

This cat has the good life. It is lying on its back completely relaxed.

Infectious Diseases

Infection	Symptoms	Communicable to humans?	Cure possible?	Vaccination possible?
Aujeszky's disease	Lack of appetite, abnormal behavior, weight loss	No	No	No
Feline immunodeficiency virus (FIV)	No specific symptoms	No	No	No
Feline infectious peritonitis (FIP)	Fever, refusal to eat, emaciation, diarrhea, vomiting, swollen abdomen	No	No	Yes
Feline leukemia virus (FeLV)	Lack of appetite, diarrhea, emaciation, abnormal behavior, swollen lymph nodes	No	No	Yes
Feline respiratory disease (FRD)	Nasal discharge, tearing, coughing, drooling, breathing difficulties, refusal to eat, dehydration	No	Yes	Yes
Feline panleuko-penia (FPL)	Apathy, watery, bloody diarrhea, vomiting, fever, pain	No	Yes	Yes
Pox virus	Pustules and ulcers on head, feet, and body	Yes	Yes	No
Rabies	Lack of appetite, weight loss, abnormal behavior	Yes	No	Yes
Skin mycosis	Hair loss, erythema, dandruff, itching, skin changes	Yes	Yes	Yes
Tetanus	Convulsions, heavy drooling, high fever	No	No	Yes
Tuberculosis	Fatigue, emaciation, fever, diarrhea, vomiting, coughing	Yes	Yes/No	No

The Sick Cat

Above all a sick cat needs warmth. Put a hot water bottle in your pet's basket.

Taking Temperature

It is best to have someone help you take your cat's temperature. One person can hold the animal's shoulders and front feet firmly, while the other takes its temperature. To do so, raise the cat's tail slightly. Insert the thermometer, lubricated with vaseline, into the rectum (see Drawing 1). Digital thermometers will give a reading after one minute, conventional thermometers take about two minutes.

The standard temperature is between 100 and 102.5°F (37.8 and 39.2°C). Below normal temperature can also be a symptom of disease.

Medications

Steambath. A steambath can be a supplemental help in alleviating the complaints of colds. Sit your cat in a transportable box and place it before a vaporizer with chamomile drops added (see Drawing 2).

Eye Drops. They can be administered as follows: hold the cat's head firmly from behind, raise it slightly, and

1. It's easier for two people to take a cat's temperature.

2. Treatment for sneezing and coughing: a steambath.

Do not touch the eyeball when giving eyedrops.

Place pills far back onto the tongue.

After giving the medicine, lightly massage the throat.

carefully pull down the lower eyelid (see Drawing 3).

Tablets. Wrap tablets in tasty morsels of food. If this method doesn't work, only the direct approach will help (see Drawing 4). Take the tablet between your thumb and forefinger. Holding the cat's head in your other hand, exert slight pressure just behind its teeth. The cat will open its mouth automatically. Now lay the tablet far back on the cat's tongue; then hold its mouth closed for a moment. As you do so, massage the cat's throat gently to make it swallow (see Drawing 5).

Liquid Medications. Administer this type of medicine with a disposable syringe, without a needle (see photo, page 76). Raise the cat's head slightly and discharge the medicine into its mouth behind the canine teeth. Squirt slowly, or the cat will choke.

Injuries Caused by Accidents

The number one danger for outdoor cats is street traffic; they also can be shot, bitten, or injured in a fall.

First Aid Procedures. A pressure dressing can stop the loss of blood from heavily bleeding wounds. Clean any sizable foreign bodies from the wound and press a piece of gauze (folded over several times) onto it. Fix the dressing in place with an elastic bandage.

With fractures, usually recognizable by the unnatural position of the limbs, put the cat in a cardboard box or in its carrier. Take the animal to the veterinarian immediately.

Poisoning

Outdoor cats are especially likely to be poisoned. The most common poisons are rodent poisons, insecticides, antifreeze, and petroleum.

Symptoms of Poisoning. Difficulty in breathing, respiratory paralysis, motor disturbances, diarrhea, vomiting, fever, cardiac arrhythmia, itching, convulsions, circulatory failure, paralysis, liver failure, nervousness, kidney failure, irritation of the gastrointestinal tract, reddening of the skin, irritation of the mucous membranes, difficulty in swallowing, pain, swelling of the skin, drooling, listlessness, and tremor.

Treatment. Poisoning should be treated only by a veterinarian.

The Love Life of Cats

Baby cats are undeniably among the cutest offspring in the animal kingdom. Uncontrolled reproduction, however, means that a miserable life is in store for many sweet little kittens.

Let us assume that a cat bears young twice a year and that four kittens out of every litter survive. These kittens continue to reproduce at the same rate. In 10 years, by these calculations, the result will be an impressive total of over 60 million cats!

The reason not all the kittens in a litter survive is that these unwanted animals perish of infections and malnutrition. In addition, about 5 or 6 million cats are destroyed in animal shelters each year. Do you want to share the responsibility for the misery of these cats? Then don't thoughtlessly abandon your domestic cat to the natural cycle of reproduction.

Neutering or Spaying and Sterilization

A female cat can be spayed when it is six months old; a male can be neutered at the age of about one year, after it has reached sexual maturity. Neutering or spaying (cast-ration) is definitely recom-mended for every cat who is not going to be used in a breeding program.

Castration refers to the surgical removal of the gonads, or reproductive glands. In a male cat, those are the testicles (neutering); in a female, the ovaries (spaying). This routine operation is performed by a veterinarian while the cat is anesthetized. As a rule, the cat recovers from this surgery without difficulty.

Once sex hormones are no longer being produced, the need to satisfy the sex drive vanishes. Cats are not aware of this absence.

Through sterilization females and males are rendered infertile only; the hormone-producing gonads (testicles and ovaries) are severed or tied off, but they remain inside the body. Sterilization has no advantages for the cat owner, because the drawbacks of sexual behavior are not eliminated (see page 84). Both males and females can contract life-threatening feline diseases (felineleukemia virus and FIP) and parasites (mites and fleas) through continuing to mate with outdoor partners after sterilization has been performed.

icture of peace and
curity. Snuggled close
ether a mother and
en take a siesta.

Breeding Pedigreed Cats

The goal of a responsible breeding program for purebred cats should always be the improvement of the breed, not mere propagation. The most important prerequisite for such an undertaking is a healthy mother cat, with the characteristics typical of her breed, who is mated with a male cat who conforms to the breed standard.

Breeding cats requires special knowledge of genetics, awareness of the right time and place for breeding, and money. In addition, you should definitely be a member of an officially recognized breed club (see Pedigreed Cat Clubs, page 87, and Useful Addresses, page 124).

Heat and Mating

The mating season of the domestic cat is February, June, and October. Among purebreds it may vary, depending on the breed.

A female cat comes into heat two or three times a year; each episode lasts three to six days. If she doesn't mate, she remains in heat for up to three weeks.

The peak of estrus is indicated by loud screaming

and rolling around on the floor. She is restless, eats less, and frequently licks her paws and genital area. If you stroke her back, she will lift her hind end into the air, lower her front end to the ground, and move her rear legs up and down without moving from the spot.

Males are ready to mate at any time if a female cat in heat is in the vicinity. The male indicates his willingness to mate by "spraying." Tail aquiver, he squirts objects with his urine. By wailing loudly, licking his penis, and running around restlessly in front of his "intended," he shows her that he is in the mood for love.

Kittens knead their mother's stomach while drinking to stimulate the flow of milk.

TIP

With the "pill" you can keep your purebred cat temporarily infertile. Hormone treatments suppress the sexual drive and the reproductive process. The pill, however, is not a long-term solution since extended hormone treatment carries with it health risks.

ama cat grooms her kittens' r tirelessly. By licking their omachs she stimulates their gestion.

During the mating act the male tries to grip the female's nape with his teeth. Once he has accomplished that, he mounts her. Soon after the penis has been inserted, the female begins to scream, while the male growls. The act of mating triggers the release of an egg by the cat's ovary.

Pregnancy and Birth

After roughly three weeks, the teats of the pregnant cat begin to turn pink and become firmer and more erect. After about thirty days—about midway through the gestation period—the little belly grows more rounded. Gestation lasts approximately sixty-three days (as few as fifty-seven or as many as seventy days would still be within the normal range). The due date is calculated on the basis of the first day of mating plus sixty-three days.

You can use a cardboard box measuring 16 × 20 inches (40 × 50 cm), about 12 inches (30 cm) high as the kittening box. Put a layer of newspapers on the bottom; then cover the papers with a clean sheet. Put the box in a quiet spot.

Shortly before giving birth, my cat scrapes and digs in her kittening box, lies down inside it, leaves and goes to her litter box, then follows me around restlessly. Then I sit down next to the kittening box and talk soothingly to the expectant mother. As the birth process begins, the cat's water (amniotic fluid) breaks. Soon afterward the first kitten appears at the birth opening, still enveloped in the fetal membrane. Then the little animal is squeezed out with powerful contractions. The mother opens the fetal envelope with her teeth, if it has not broken open on its own. She licks her genitals painstakingly and consumes the afterbirth, which appears after a few more contractions. After the mother cat has severed the umbilical cord, she licks the wet newborn dry. The kittens are born at intervals of half an hour or an hour.

If the Mother Has Insufficient Milk

Sometimes the mother cat, or queen, fails to produce milk. A surrogate is the simplest solution to the problem of feeding the kittens. Unfortunately, a suitable mother cat cannot always be found right away.

85

Hand-rearing is time-consuming and stressful. In any event, you need to have a supply of queen's milk replacement (from the pet store) on hand when the due date approaches. If there is a need for it, pour the milk replacement into a nursing bottle (available in pet stores) and feed the little kittens every two hours—at night as well. After every feeding, massage their little tummies with a paper tissue, so that feces and urine will be voided.

A New Home for the Kittens

A cat bears an average of one to eight kittens per litter, rarely more. If the litter is a large one, you certainly will not wish to keep all the kittens. They should go to their new homes at the age of approximately twelve weeks, after they have been vaccinated twice (see Vaccination Schedule, page 74). Kittens that are separated from their mother earlier than that will often be delayed in their development.

For domestic kittens, it is often difficult to find a home where they will be treated well. Give the kittens only to people whom you know and who are reliable and fond of animals.

A purebred cat can be advertised for sale in a specialized periodical, an illustrated magazine that features animals, or a daily newspaper. A good pedigreed cat club will also have a kitten placement office. Sometimes pet stores also will be glad to help place pedigreed cats. When you sell a pedigreed cat, you should always draw up a purchase a g r e e m e n t (see page 28).

This tomcat quickly recoils to get away from the other cat.

What Happens in the First Few Weeks of a Kitten's Life?

A kitten comes into the world blind and deaf. Immediately the little one seeks its way to the milk source, its mother's teats. It can already smell keenly. Seven days later the kitten has doubled its birth weight. It now weighs about 7 ounces (200 grams).

Now its development proceeds very rapidly. Around the tenth day after birth, the kitten opens its eyes. At approximately three weeks it makes its first attempt to investigate its surroundings. After about four weeks it has a complete set of baby teeth. The kitten can now tear at tiny pieces of meat.

During its fourth and fifth weeks the kitten learns by playing with its siblings and mother all that it will need later in life. It learns for example how to catch and kill mice and how to climb up a tree. Now it is time for the kitten to come into contact with humans. Young cats who have no contact with humans at this time, often remain forever shy. At twelve weeks the kitten is independent enough to survive without its mother or siblings.

What Can a Pedigreed Cat Club Offer?

A pedigreed cat club offers exchange of breeders' experiences in meetings and articles in specialized publications, lectures, and advice on all matters related to breeding, genetics, and the care and nutrition of cats. They also provide placement and documentation of breeding-qualified adult and young animals, documentation of top-quality breeding studs, organization of cat shows, maintenance of a stud book, issuance of pedigrees, exchange with foreign breeder organizations, and training of breeders as show judges.

Beautiful Cats on Exhibit

When a cat is judged at these shows—by a trained show judge who follows internationally accepted guidelines—the breeder is given information about the merits and defects of his or her animal. International shows usually are held on weekends and generally last for two days.

The purpose of a show, however, is to give breeders an overview of the current status of breeding programs and to enable them to compare their cats with others.

Understanding Your Pet and Keeping It Occupied

If you want to develop a harmonious relationship with your cat, you need to know a great deal about it, understand its nature, and spend a lot of time with it.

Cats make the best playing partners— but only for as long as they want to play.

The Cat's Abilities

For its way of life as a hunter in the wild, a cat needs an agile, powerful body that reacts quickly and extremely keen sensory capabilities.

The Cat's Body

Build. The skeleton lends the body stability and protects vital organs from injury. Its construction enables the tendons (connected to muscles that contract and relax) to move the bones in the joints reciprocally so that the cat develops enormous speed and momentum.

Skin and Coat. The skin that covers the body protects the organism like a cloak. By sweating, it regulates the water balance in the body and the body temperature. In addition, nerve cells located in the skin transmit information— the sensation of pain, for example—to the brain. The coat is excellent protection against cold and damp.

Feet, Claws, and Tail. A cat has five toes on its front feet and four on the hind feet. The needle-sharp claws on the front paws are retracted into pockets of skin when the cat walks. In this way the claws are protected and kept sharp. The claws on the hind feet, however, cannot be retracted, and over time they are worn down. The cat's locomotor system and the soft cushions of the balls on its soles give it its soft gait. The tail helps the cat keep its balance when it jumps or falls.

Teeth. The cat's set of thirty teeth is designed for eating meat. The large canine, or corner, teeth (two above and two below), which curve slightly inward, are quite noticeable. The cat uses them to hold its prey firmly. The molars, with their scissor movement, help the cat to grind its prey into small pieces. The cat's set of teeth is not completely developed until the age of seven to nine months.

The rough tongue is covered with horny papillae to loosen the meat from the bones of the prey. It is also an excellent tool for coat care.

The Cat's Senses

Good hearing, sight, and touch are extremely important prerequisites for successful hunting.

Hearing. The cat's two large, wide-flared, movable auricles are outward and visible signs of its excellent hearing. A cat is able to detect and accurately

fter a nap the cat does
xtensive stretching exercises.
his way the circulation comes
ack into gear.

locate the tiniest noises of its prey at a great distance. It hears tones in the frequency range of 65 kHz, while a human's ability to hear stops at 20 kHz.

Sight. The cat's visual faculty is very well developed. Using its large, light-sensitive eyes, it can make out its hunting objective clearly and advance toward its prey unerringly. At dusk, its pupils open wide to let it use the dim light to the utmost. In bright light, on the other hand, the pupils contract.

Smell. The cat's sense of smell is not extremely well developed.

Taste. The sense of taste is not very pronounced. Food preferences are more apt to be based on habit.

Touch. The cat receives sensory stimuli through its highly sensitive tactile hairs, including those above its eyes, and its whiskers (vibrissae). They help it get its bearings. These hairs function as "antennas" with which they orient themselves quite well.

How Cats Behave

Since the cat does not understand our language, it concentrates on the move-ments, body attitude, and voice of its human. Many cats can "understand" their human partner so well that some cat owners believe in telepathy. If the human behaves according

Top: Something has awakene the cat's interest.
Bottom: Meowing and still in a friendly mood.

**p: Displeasure. Ears spread to
e sides, enlarged pupils.
ottom: Distinct threatening
havior. Next comes the attack.**

cat's facial expressions, body attitude, and tail position.

Some of the cat's modes of behavior toward humans are derived from its innate grooming instinct, its natural behavior toward its mother as a young kitten, and its sexual behavior.

Behavioral Patterns That You Need to Recognize

Establishing Friendly Contact. The cat does this by rubbing its cheek or nape against a human's legs and nestling against him or her, holding its head up to rub, and licking the hands or face of "its" human.

Irritable Mood. The telltale signs include slapping the ground with its tail, crouching and laying its ears back, hissing, and bristling its fur.

Licking. During the first few weeks, the mother cat licks the anal region of her babies thoroughly. It is this "massage" that enables the kittens to void feces and urine.

A male cat will lick little kittens, as well as the female he is courting, as a proof of his affection.

Licking a human's face and hands is a friendly gesture that stems from the grooming instinct and the sex drive.

to the cat's expectations, he or she will win the cat's attachment in every possible way.

You can quickly find out what mood your pet happens to be in by closely observing your

Kneading. By kneading, or pressing its paws alternately against its mother's teats, a kitten stimulates her flow of milk. Behaving this way toward a human is to be interpreted as a sign of profound trust.

Purring. The cat shows its happiness and contentment by purring. Purring offers no evidence that the animal is in good health, however, since sick animals also purr. Even little kittens purr quite early in life, when they are suckling contentedly at their mother's teat.

Rolling Around. The cat also displays its natural sexual behavior toward humans. It will turn its rear end toward someone and roll back and forth on the ground.

Playing. When playing, a cat tries out social behavior and fighting behavior (fights involving rivalry, for example). It uses its mother, litter mates, and prey (such as mice and rats) as playmates, but it will also happily accept a human playmate.

Fear and Resistance. Usually when a tame cat displays this behavior with a human, it is attributable to improper behavior on the human's part.

Defense and offense are anxiety reactions in a hopeless situation where flight has become impossible. If a human drives a cat into a corner, for

Left: The kitten practices handling its prey.

94

cat encounter: Both
approach one another
refully. After some sniffing
ch goes on its own way.

example, locks it in a cage, or holds it tightly, the cat feels threatened. First it will hiss; then it will lunge and use its teeth and claws.

Acts of aggression occur among cats too; there are cat fights and territorial disputes that sometimes end in bloodshed.

Prey-catching Instinct. The cat is a predatory animal. The longer it is deprived of an opportunity to act out its drive to catch prey, the lower its stimulus threshold becomes. When playing with a little ball, it will react with keen intentness, just as it does when playing with a mouse. If the ball rolls away, the cat is compelled to race after it and try repeatedly to catch it. Even the familiar hand of its owner,

95

Rare animal friendship: The kitten is dreaming in its hammock just not about mice

if it moves fast enough, is a substitute for prey. Be careful when you play with your cat; you might get scratched.

Flight Behavior. If the cat has gotten out of the house, under no circumstances should you immediately run after it to recapture it. The cat does not have great staying power as a runner. After a short distance it will seek cover as quickly as possible. Stay right where you are, keeping your eye on the cat until it interrupts its flight and remains in one position. Then you can approach it

slowly and carefully, acting as if you didn't even see it. Once you are close to the cat, talk to it in a quiet voice; try to pet it, moving your hand slowly; and then catch it.

Of course, you could just wait for your cat to come home. Doing so, however, leaves the animal at risk of being hit by a car, being stolen, or ingesting poison.

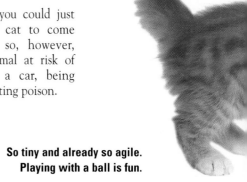

So tiny and already so agile. Playing with a ball is fun.

Why Does a Cat Need Whiskers?

Perhaps you have asked yourself why your cat can balance itself so agilely on the windowsill without tipping anything over. It can also recognize exactly if a door opening is wide enough to get through.

A cat can do this with the help of its whiskers. They act as antennas and tell the cat even in the dark, if an obstacle stands in the way. It is amazing that the cat doesn't even have to touch the obstacle with its whiskers. They pick up even the slightest change in the air. The flow of air is different where an obstacle stands, than where the cat can go unimpeded.

Cats have touchhair on the face, on the cheeks, over the eyes, on the nose, under the chin, and even on the back side of its front legs. A cat whose whiskers are damaged can no longer find its way about in its environment. It is as if it were suddenly blind.

Often cat mothers snip the whiskers of their youngsters off when cleaning them. We do not know why they do this. The little kittens can do without these whiskers in the beginning and later they grow in again naturally.

Getting the Cat Settled Properly

You have to struggle develop any good relatio ship, including that betwe human and cat. Only lovi devotion and understandi will create over time the rig climate between you and yc pet. When your new hou mate joins the househo you'll need empathy a patience. The first few da will decide whether the c develops trust and confiden in you.

The First Hours at Home

It is best to bring your c home by car and to ta another person with yc Then one of you can ta soothingly to the cat on t ride home.

Transport the cat in special pet carrier (see pa 50). Have the cat's breeder previous owner give you sor used kitty litter and a sma amount of your new pet's usu food. That will make t adjustment easier for the cat

When you get home ta the carrier into a quiet roo

A cat lies on its back only when it feels completely safe and sound.

98

ogs and cats can also live ogether peacefully. If they row up together there is arely a problem.

open it, and let the cat explore its new environment in peace and quiet.

For the time being, all the family members need to keep as still as possible and let the cat do as it likes.

Let the cat decide when it wants to make contact with its new human family and to allow itself to be petted. Never hold the animal tightly against its will or drag it out from under furniture with force.

During the first few hours, do not leave your new pet alone.

Going Out in the Yard

Before the cat is allowed to go out in the yard, it has to be completely familiar with your home and to regard it as the center of its sphere of life. That will take about two weeks. Then you can open the door to the yard slightly and allow the cat to enlarge its territory gradually.

At first the door has to be left open while the cat is out. If it gets frightened, it should be able to retreat into the safety of its familiar sphere at any time.

99

Many older animals that have been spayed or neutered prefer to stay near their familiar home. Male cats, sometimes even neutered ones, are more inclined to stake out a wider territory than female cats.

If your house is near a heavily traveled street, you should consider keeping the cat indoors all the time, to protect it from the danger of an accident.

If your house is located near fields, meadows, and woods, the risk of being run over is lower, but the cat might get into a hunting area. Some hunters are very keen on shooting cats that are running loose outdoors. They view them as hunting rivals. If the hunters are local residents, sometimes it helps to have a personal talk with them and introduce your cat.

Getting Cats Used to Each Other

It is easiest to get two young animals accustomed to one another. As a rule, putting a young cat together with an older one presents few problems. Things become more difficult when you want to get two adult feline individualists to live together in peace. In any event, you have to allow

What Cats Like

What a Cat Likes	What a Cat Dislikes
● A little place in the sun, near the stove, on the sofa, in the bed, atop the cupboard	● A lonely life without contact, as an abandoned stray or kept in isolation
● Several times a day, a "chat" with its owner or with other cats	● Food that is too cold or too hot or that has gone bad in dirty bowls
● Eating together with the family, or being given a sample of foods now and then	● Being combed when it has other important plans at the moment, or having matted knots of hair pulled out with force
● Being brushed and combed gently, but only when the cat is in the mood for it	● Marital disputes, screaming children, barking dogs, car and tractor noise, low-flying planes, noisy New Year's Eve parties, and thunderstorms
● Quiet voices, friendly and gentle	● People who disregard cats or are afraid of them
● Visitors who try to win over the cat or bring it a little something	● Being treated as a decorative piece of furniture
● Now and then catching a mouse, chasing chickens, startling its owner, annoying birds, playing with paper in little balls or rolls	● Being shooed away from the place where it was sleeping
● Sleeping undisturbed for hours on end	● Being excluded from parts of the house
● Doing acrobatics atop tall pieces of furniture or between glasses and vases, climbing curtains, sharpening claws on sofa and wallpaper	● Rainy weather, the cold with no chance to get warm
	● Dandruffy hair, greasy, matted hair on its coat, biting ticks, fleas, ear mites

them plenty of time for the adjustment period.

At first, protect the newcomer from the established cat with a latticed gate (in the doorway between two rooms, for example). Once the two cats approach each other peaceably through the gate, you can try putting them together—under supervision.

Cats and Other Pets

If other animals already live in your home, you have to get the new arrival used to them gradually. It is, however, impossible to predict if the cat will get along with the other animals. There have even been friendships between a cat and mouse. That is surely an exception to the rule.

101

The cat waits intently for its food. It begs for food and attention by rubbing its head against your leg.

Cats and dogs definitely can live together quite peaceably and even develop friendships. Nevertheless, at first they will have difficulties in communicating, because of their different ways of life and ingrained forms of expression. Two young animals of these different species usually adjust quite well to each other. An adult dog, if well-trained and devoted to its master, can be trained at least to tolerate the cat and to observe a truce. Do not let the animals be together without supervision until things have reached that point.

Rabbits, small rodents, and birds are all prey for cats. For a cat that acts largely on instinctive impulse, these animals are often a real "taste treat." Only rarely can a cat and its potential prey live together in harmony—and there will always be a risk. Keep the cat at a distance by placing the endangered pets in a separate room or in secure cages.

Cats and Children

Nowadays the educational value for children of having a cat is indisputable. A cat makes not only a fine playmate for an older child, but can be a

TIP

If your child wants to take sole responsibility for the cat, the child should be at least of school age. Before that time children cannot accept the responsibility for an animal.

With a swagger and raised tail the cat rubs against the leg and purrs.

devoted friend as well. However, a cat must also be cared for. It needs regular feedings and fresh water, and the litter box must be cleaned. A child can learn very early to accept responsibility and to respect the needs of another living thing.

The calming effect of a cat on a child can also be observed. Nervous, fidgety, or aggressive children are frequently calmer and more balanced in their behavior.

If you are knowledgeable about your pet's care and observe certain rules of good hygiene, a cat will present virtually no health hazard.

To rule out all danger of an accident, however, you should not leave infants or small children and cats together unsupervised.

A cat is not a good playmate, however, for a small child. As discussed on page 25, a young child can sometimes be too rough with the cat. This can lead to the cat striking out with its claws to defend itself, leading to an unpleasant situation at the least and possibly a dangerous situation.

If a young cat and a child are playing, make sure that the child does not make excessive demands on the cat. Young cats do not realize on their own that too much is being asked of them, and children are not good judges of that either.

Training Program for an Independent Pet

Assuming that your cat trusts you, it can learn to respect your wishes.

Basic Rules of Cat Training:

■ Patience. Don't assume that you can correct the cat once or twice and then expect it in the future to refrain from the prohibited behavior.

■ Consistency. Don't forbid your cat to do something one day and then generously overlook the same behavior the next day.

■ Authority. When you tell your cat not to do something, say "No" in a loud voice.

■ Same words. Always use the same words and expressions for training your pet.

■ Reward. Praise your cat with positive motivation when it has done something right. Punishments such as blows will destroy whatever trust the cat has developed.

Answering to Its Name

Cats readily answer to names that end in an "i" sound (ee or y). To get your cat used to its name, call it by name whenever you feed it or pet it, especially at the beginning of its training. If you ever scold your pet, never use its name during the process.

Often a squirt of lemon juice is enough to discourage the cat from stealing.

With a spray of water from the plant mister you can keep your cat from climbing on the plants or nibbling at them.

Breaking Your Pet of Bad Habits

Does your cat go fishing in your aquarium, swipe food from the table, or sharpen its claws on your best furniture? A surprise often helps in these cases, especially with "repeat offenders." A sudden stream of water coming from behind—from a plant mister, for example—will give the cat a real fright. Tossing a light aluminum chain directly next to the cat, or a strong current of air from a bellows also will divert it from its undesirable actions. However, it is essential to make sure that the cat does not draw a connection between you and the unpleasant surprise. Otherwise, you

risk losing your cat's trust, as already mentioned.

Getting Used to the Cat Leash

Pet stores offer special cat leashes with a chest harness. Cats are not exactly enthusiastic about this kind of restraint, but a cat leash can come in handy—for example, if you live on a heavily traveled street but want to let your pet enjoy some exercise outdoors without danger.

Here are some tips for helping your cat get used to the leash.

Step One: Let the cat play with the leash and harness for a few days to become familiar with them.

Step Two: Put the chest harness on the cat for only a few minutes. Then put the harness on for longer periods of time, to get it used to the device.

Step Three: Next, fasten the leash to the chest harness and coax the cat toward you with a toy. This will familiarize it with the tug of the leash. Once it "yields to its fate" and accepts the leash, shower the cat with praise.

Step Four: Practice outdoors with the leash and harness.

Great Ideas for Playing with Your Cat

Several references have been made in this book to the importance of play in a cat's life. Indoor cats are especially eager for "their" humans to find time, at last, to play with them.

Keeping It Busy

A cat that lives exclusively indoors, with no other cat to keep it company, does not have enough to do unless you spend plenty of time with it each day.

You should set aside at least one hour a day for a single indoor cat; having "its" human around all day is best for the cat.

Singles who work outside the home should spend their evening largely at home with their cat. If you don't have the time, it is better to acquire two cats simultaneously (see page 20).

When you and your pet play, always remember not to use your own hand as an object of play; you could easily be injured (see Important Note, page 127). Use your hand only for petting your cat.

Teaching It Little Tricks

Many cats love learning little tricks that provide enjoyment for them, since it entails diversion and variety. It is not animal training in the conventional sense because the cats will not participate unless they want to.

The prerequisites for this kind of training are daily practice, and, of course, the cat has to enjoy it as well. If you notice that your pet is no longer attentive, don't force it to participate. That would destroy the cat's trust in you (see page 104).

Praise your cat after every little trick and reward your pet with a treat.

Sitting Up on Its Hind Legs

With the cat in a seated position, hold out a treat—a little piece of cheese, for example—in front of the cat's mouth when it is seated. Raise the piece of cheese higher and higher, until the cat draws itself up. When it is sitting on its hind legs, give it its reward and say "Up!"

Repeat this command each time, until the cat has learned the trick.

Hold a feather or a ball in the air: your cat will leap after the "prey."

Play catch. Cats have a highly developed need for play. Playing is only really interesting, however, with a partner.

Retrieving

There are some cats that are passionately fond of fetching, without ever having been taught to do so, probably because of their instinctual impulse to carry prey back to young kittens in the nest. If your cat comes leaping toward you bringing its little ball or a fur-fabric mouse, it probably is one of the "gifted" cats. Impatiently it will stare at you and wait for you to throw the object once more. You can use the command "Fetch!" to encourage the cat and invite it to begin the game anew. Incidentally, retrieving will also work when you have company. Dog owners are often very impressed if you can

Nothing will come of looking at a picture book. The kitten wants to play and the children will readily agree.

What Do Cats Really Like?

Your cat loves for you to rub its coat softly and to scratch between its ears or under its chin. You simply have to observe your cat carefully. It will show you when it wants to be spoiled. It will come to you with its tail raised and rub its head against your leg.

Cats also like to play with you. They will, for example, chase after ping pong balls or wooden spools of yarn or "hunt" after stuffed mice. Be sure that the toys are not too small so that your cat doesn't swallow them. The cat will normally decide when to put an end to the playing. Little kittens, however, don't know when they are tired, so you should not overdo playing with them.

get your cat to demonstrate its ability to retrieve.

Learning to "Talk"

Yes, you read that correctly; you can get a cat to speak. Hold a piece of food under your cat's nose and ask, "Who wants something to eat?" Usually—especially if it happens to be hungry—it will look longingly at the food and say "meow, meo, me."

Jump!

Teaching a cat to jump is not at all difficult. When you see the cat sitting in front of a chair, a sofa, or the bed, pat the furniture. If the cat starts to jump, give the command "Jump." Once it is up, give it a little piece of food as a reward. Soon the cat will jump up upon hearing the command "Jump!" even if it wasn't contemplating doing so, because it expects to be given a morsel of food.

Balancing

When wandering through their territory in the wild, cats perform a number of daredevil balancing acts along narrow eaves or the top of a garden fence.

Balancing can also be simulated inside your home, for example, with a wooden lath placed between two chairs. Put the cat on one of the supporting chairs and use a treat to coax it to cross over the lath to the other chair. It is important that the lath be placed securely and not wobble when the cat walks across it; otherwise, the trick will never work. The cautious cat will

TIP

Do not leave the following things for your cat to play with unless you are watching; they can cause injury: balls of wool, nonelastic cords and ribbons, rubber bands, soft plastic pieces, little balls from newspaper, or aluminum foil.

The kitten has hidden itself under a newspaper roof and is encouraging with its meows more things to do.

also refuse to use shaky, unsteady scratching posts more than once (see page 51).

Jumping Through a Hoop

What lions and tigers learn in the circus, your kitty can learn in your home: how to jump through a hoop. Hold the hoop, touching the floor, in front of the cat. Holding a little treat on the opposite side of the hoop, coax the cat to step through it. Bit by bit, keep raising the hoop a little higher in the air. Always use the command "Jump!" when the cat leaps through the hoop. Then give your pet its reward.

Fun with Ball Games

Many cats can make truly acrobatic leaps after a ball tossed into the air. Cats also like the so-called "dangle toys" (buy them in pet stores or make them yourself). A short string is attached to the end of a stick, and from the string is suspended a little ball with a bell or simply a ball of paper. Hold the little ball in front of the cat's nose and move it upward or sideways. The cat

ily play time: The young
yssinian reaches excitedly
m its carton for the red
ather.

will hit at the ball with its paw and try to catch it.

Hiding

Cats love all kinds of "caves" and "hollows," including an open drawer or an open suitcase. Cats also like to slip into a cardboard box in which you have cut a few holes in the side of the box to enter and exit. A tent made of newspaper (see photo, left) or empty round detergent containers can also be used to play hide-and-seek.

"Chase"

Crouch down on the ground and cautiously creep toward the cat. With its keen hearing, it will detect your motion at once and swiftly take cover, whether it be an armchair or the couch. There it will "lurk," the tip of its tail quivering from excitement, until you reappear in its field of vision. Then it will most assuredly take to its heels. You follow it, but only for a short distance; then it is your turn to hide. You will see; the kitty will wait awhile, then come back to see what has happened to you. After all, it is curious. The cat quickly learns that this is an enjoyable game and will never tire of playing it.

111

Problems and How to Solve Them

Abnormal behavior is rare in cats, and it usually is the fault of human errors in dealing with the cat. Even less common is a pathological disturbance of behavior.

Shy Cats

Possible Causes. Cats may be shy because of bad experiences with humans or a genetic predisposition (nature of a wild animal).

Remedies. If the cat associates humans with bad experiences, it may become shy, fearful, or aggressive. Infinite patience and devotion are needed if an animal of this kind is to develop trust in humans again. If the cat has a genetic predisposition to shyness, only slight progress can be made, even with much patience.

Divide the cat's daily ration of food into small portions, and feed it directly from your hand several times a day. Stretching your hand far out, squat down and wait for the shy animal to approach. The smell of the food and talking quietly to the cat may be helpful here. Under no circumstances should you run after a shy cat, try to catch it, or hold it tightly.

Cats That Scratch and Bite

Possible Causes. Cat owners often use their bare hands when they play fighting and prey-catching games with their pets. The cat will then regard the hand as a substitute prey object, and it will sink its teeth into it (as with a mouse).

Sometimes cats that have grown up in a household with small children have had bad experiences, and they will defend themselves by scratching and biting.

Remedy. If the cat plays wildly and scratches and bites, you need to make it clear that such behavior is too rough. Stop the game at once—without punishing your pet—and walk away. Sometimes the cat will also stop if you "wail" loudly. The same applies if the cat uses its sharp claws to climb up people's legs and clothes.

If Your Pet Soils

Possible Causes. Your cat may soil because it is a marking behavior of sexually mature cats, it has an intestinal or urinary tract infection, or

the litter box is in a b location—for example, n to a high-traffic area or next its food bowl.

Other potential causes that there is too little litter the cat's box, the cat does like the brand of litter, the b is too small, the roof (w enclosed litter boxes) is low or the portal is too sm the litter box is not cleaned a regular basis, or the litter b smells of disinfectant. Ot causes include changes in cat's life, such as moving t new home or sudde banning the cat from go into certain parts of the hou

The intrusion of n housemates into the c sphere (second cat, spouse partner, baby, dog), appearance of tensions wh several cats are kept, a arguments between hum can also disturb the c mental equilibrium.

Remedies. The male c habit of spraying to mark territory can be eliminated having him neutered (see p 82). If there is a patholog disorder, only the veterina can help.

Unexplained soiling pla great demands on the owner's powers of empathy

First, the cat's box has to be [ma]de as attractive as possible. [Fil]l it to a depth of 4 inches [(10] cm) with a brand of litter [tha]t the cat will accept, and [cha]nge the litter daily (for [som]e cats, several times a [day]). Some cats prefer to use [lar]ge, uncovered tubs as a [toi]let, but most will accept [box]elike cat boxes.

If all these approaches fail [and] the cat persists in using [one] or more places in your [hom]e to deposit its excrement, [try] the following: put litter [box]es at the places the cat [pre]fers and get the cat used to [the]m in this way, change the

floor covering, or set up the food and water bowls at the soiled spot. Cats will normally not do their "business" in the vicinity of their food and water.

■ There is also the possibility of counterconditioning as a way to keep the cat away from places where it misbehaves. If you catch your cat in the act, spray deodorant on its nose. It will loathe that. Finally, spray the spot you want to keep the cat away from with the same scent but do not choose a scent that you yourself use.

■ Some cats prefer certain surfaces for doing their "business," such as newspaper, freshly washed laundry, bed sheets, carpet mats, and plastic bags. It is possible to place these materials in the cat's toilet and gradually replace them with litter.

■ If all your efforts fail, you have only one remaining possibility: get the cat used to going outdoors at times or give it away to someone—a farm family, for example—who will keep it as an outdoor cat exclusively.

The Cat Is Too Fat

Possible Causes. A cat can be too fat because it suffers from a lack of movement (mostly cats in apartments are the victims); it gets too much to eat; the cat suffers from an excessive appetite, which is probably caused by a behavioral problem; or it has been spayed or neutered, which can result in the cat's being calmer and balanced, due to the cat's lack of sex and reproductive drive. Some cats tend to put on weight after spaying or neutering; in very rare cases a metabolic illness or some certain medications can cause obesity.

Kittens learn to use the litter box by imitating their mother.

113

Remedies. A housecat needs enough opportunities for climbing and playing and, of course, interacting with its "humans" who regularly take time to play and fool with it. If a cat eats too much, you can first reduce the portions a bit. Offer the cat some of those items not on its favorite foods list. If it really is hungry, it will eat this "lousy" food too. There are special diets that you can obtain from a veterinarian. As a precaution you should pay attention to your cat's diet so that it receives well-balanced meals and proper nutrition. Do not spoil your darling with little snacks between meals or feed it from your own dinner table. Severe overweight can harm your cat because it puts stress on the heart, the circulatory system, and the joints. In addition, it decreases its life expectancy.

The Cat Is Picky

Possible Causes. The cat was fed with a certain type of food as a youngster and has become so accustomed to it that later it will only eat this type of food; the cat regularly gets some-

thing to nibble on in between meals and soon will eat nothing else; the cat connects with a certain type of food some unpleasant experience (a bitter medication not completely mixed in, the food was spoiled) and will refuse it in the future; the cat takes its food only from "its" person and from its feeding bowl in the usual place.

Remedies. Even little kittens should be acquainted with a variety of flavors of store-bought food, then later they will not reject it. Your cat should receive little treats between

meals only as an exception that it does not refuse its ma meal. And if the cat is not excited about the meal, ther is not very hungry. Do r offer it something e immediately.

Monotonous feeding unhealthy. Either an und or oversupply of necessa elements can lead to hea problems. To acclimate yc cat to a balanced diet prepared foods, mix a bit o every day into the ca favorite foods, until t prepared food increases to t point where the cat is eati only it.

If someone else will have feed and care for yc cat for a while, is advisable have the c

The cat taps at the midget hamster. Living together with this animal of prey is not without some risk.

el comfortable with this person beforehand. Then it ill not turn down the food.

The Cat Begs or Steals Food

Possible Causes. A cat may beg steal food because it is hungry; it is not fed on a gular schedule; the aroma of "people food" is too enticing; e cat is very dependent and ants a "sign of affection," mething from the plate; or e cat is simply curious.

Remedies. Feed your cat at e same time that you are ving your meal so that it will ot have to watch the meal ing hungry. It is important to here to a regular schedule of eal times, preferably in the orning and the evening. If u simply bar the cat from ur eating place, it will view is as a punishment.

When the cat begs even hen not hungry, only some sciplinary measure will help. it springs onto the table or shes itself constantly and mandingly against you, tell a clear "No." Always use e same short command d combine it with some pleasant experience, for example, blowing at it. Never leave food remains lying about, in a tidy kitchen the cat will find nothing to steal.

Maybe you should pay a little more attention and devotion so that you do not have to resort to this substitute of giving in.

The Cat Always Sucks at Clothing

Possible Causes. Sucking is an infantile behavior of all mammals. Many cats never abandon this behavior. This has nothing to do with whether it was removed from its mother early. They simply like to suck on something as they did with their mother when they were babies. It provides a sense of well being and security.

Remedies. If this behavior is constant and annoys you, you can spray or paint the favorite sucking spot with something that smells unpleasant, for example, with deodorant.

The Cat Is Restless and Wants to Go Outside

Possible Causes. A restless cat could be an unneutered or unspayed cat. Male cats especially are freedom loving and restless in an apartment. Sexually mature female cats also sometimes wander restlessly about in the search for a partner. A kitten that has a free barn cat as a mother and has grown up wild will not be accustomed to living exclusively in an apartment.

Remedies. You should spay or neuter adult cats (see p. 82).

Before you acquire a cat, learn where the cat comes from and whether or not this is a pure domestic cat. A cat that was previously used to running outside will be difficult to retrain. Otherwise, your only choice is to engage yourself intensively with the cat in order to distract it from the desire to go outdoors during this acclimation period. A cat must have the opportunity to play itself out. If you have a garden, you can later train it for this limited outside activity (see p. 99).

The Cat Roams and Does Not Come Home

Possible Causes. Cats may roam when they are not tightly bound to the home or when

115

they were allowed to roam freely around their birthplace where they were kept unrestrained. You may also be dealing with a sexually active animal that is neither spayed nor neutered, and it is quite normal for such an animal to search out a sexual partner, and to scout out and defend its territory.

Remedies. It is relatively simple to train a spayed or neutered animal to have regulated comings and goings. The primary requirement is that the cat responds to its name (see p. 104) and responds to being called home immediately. A single specific sound can be very helpful in this regard, for example, shaking the food bowl. When the hungry cat does come home, you should give it a

small snack as a reward. Naturally it is also very important that the cat has an evening meal at a specific time. The actual time is less important here than the onset of dusk. When the cat is occupied eating, you should then close the door and soon it will be used to this evening ritual.

The Cat Catches Birds

Possible Causes. Cats are [?] called predators and it is [?] their nature to capture and [?] little rodents and birds. In t[?] way they nourish themsel[?] only when no human provid[?] food for them. This behav[?] has nothing to do with cruel[?] If, however, your cat is t[?] dedicated to its hunting dri[?] the reason may be that it [?] no opportunities to satisfy [?] urges.

Remedies. Play a lot w[?] your cat, encourage it to r[?] and jump and hunt and offe[?] a replacement object of p[?] such as a ball or a stuf[?] mouse. This way it c[?] somewhat satisfy its hunti[?] and predatory drive a[?] possibly will not hunt so mu[?] when outdoors. Avoid putt[?] up a bird house when there [?] lots of cats in your gard[?] running around, or sec[?] them with the help of fenci[?] If necessary you must ke[?]

First acquaintance: The cat paws the young puppy. First it must slowly get used to him.

our cat indoors during the birds' mating season (May and June). A cat can catch a healthy adult bird only in the rarest of cases.

The Cats Don't Get Along with Each Other

Possible Causes. Cats may not get along if they are sexually mature, unspayed or unneutered animals that, in addition, live in too cramped quarters. Unneutered male cats, in particular, based on their natural rivalry never live together in close quarters. The defense of one's own territory is an inborn instinct that can be more or less developed. It also happens that cats who have been living together peacefully for a long time will suddenly be aggressive to one another, which leads to bloody battles; both animals, for unexplained reasons, cannot tolerate one another any longer.

Remedies. Adult animals who will not be used for breeding should be spayed or neutered (see page 82). In addition, the more space that is made available to the cats, the less aggressive they will be, since all animals have enough opportunity for retreat. You cannot simply place another cat "before the nose" of an old, long-time resident cat. You should protect the new one; even when it is not a young kitten. The newcomer might be more easily accepted if you used a fence. This way the cats can see, smell, and hear each other and make their first contacts. After a few days when they have become acquainted, then you can try to let the cats be together under your watchful eye. There are cats who can never be made to accept one another, since there is an individual enmity between the animals that one simply must accept. In this case you will have to find a new home for one of the two animals.

My Cat

Place a favorite photo here.

Name

Born on

Breeder   Spayed/neutered on

Sex

Tattoo number/transponder

Breed/color

Eye color   Weight as of

Distinguishing characteristics

Favorite food(s)

What's Typical of My Cat

Veterinarian's name and address

Eight-week-old Norwegian Forest cat.

**Wild color Somali ten
months old.**

USEFUL ADDRESSES AND LITERATURE

North American Cat Registries

American Association of Cat Enthusiasts (AACE)
P.O. Box 213
Pine Brook, NJ 07058
(201) 335-6717

American Cat Association (ACA)
8101 Katherine Avenue
Panorama City, CA 91402
(818) 781-5656

American Cat Fanciers Association (ACFA)
P.O. Box 203
Point Lookout, MO 65726
(417) 334-5430

Canadian Cat Association (CCA)
220 Advance Boulevard, Suite 101
Brampton, Ontario
Canada L6T 4J5
(905) 459-1481

Cat Fanciers' Association (CFA)
1805 Atlantic Avenue
P.O. Box 1005
Manasquan, NJ 08736-0805
(908) 528-9797

Cat Fanciers' Federation (CFF)
Box 661
Gratis, OH 45330
(513) 787-9009

National Cat Fanciers' Association (NCFA)
20305 West Burt Road
Brant, MI 48614
(517) 585-3179

The International Cat Association (TICA)
P.O. Box 2684
Harlingen, TX 78551
(210) 428-8046

United Feline Organization (UFO)
P.O. Box 3234
Olympia, WA 98509-3234
(360) 438-6903

Other Associations

American Humane Society
P.O. Box 1266
Denver, CO 80201
(303) 695-0811

American Society for the Prevention of Cruelty to Animals (ASPCA)
424 East 92nd Street
New York, NY 10128
(212) 876-7700

Cornell Feline Health Center
Cornell University College of Veterinary Medicine
Ithaca, NY 14853
(607) 253-3414

The Delta Society
P.O. Box 1080
Renton, WA 98057
(206) 226-7357

Tortoise-shell Maine Coon kitten, five weeks old.

he Humane Society of the
   United States (HSUS)
00 L Street, NW
ashington, DC 20037
02) 452-1100

orris Animal Foundation
Inverness Drive, East
glewood, CO 80112-5480
00) 243-2345

et Protection Services

ATOO-A-Pet
71 S.W. 20th Court
rt Lauderdale, FL 33317
otline: (800) 828-8667
ffice: (954) 581-5834

ational Dog Registry
. Box 116
oodstock, NY 12498
otline: (800) 637-3647
ffice: (914) 679-2355

at Magazines

ATS *Magazine*
bscriptions:
. Box 420240
lm Coast, FL 32142-0240
04) 445-2818
itorial offices:
. Box 290037
rt Orange, FL 32129-0037
04) 788-2770

Cat Fancy
Subscriptions:
P.O. Box 52864
Boulder, CO 80322-2864
(303) 666-8504
Editorial offices:
P.O. Box 6050
Mission Viejo, CA 92690
(714) 855-8822

Cat Fancier's Almanac
Cat Fanciers' Association
1805 Atlantic Avenue
P.O. Box 1005
Manasquan, NJ 08736-0805
(908) 528-9797

Catnip (newsletter)
Tufts University School of
   Veterinary Medicine
Subscriptions:
P.O. Box 420014
Palm Coast, FL 32142-0014
(800) 829-0926
Editorial offices:
300 Atlantic Street, 10th
   Floor
Stamford, CT 06901
(203) 353-6650

Cat World
10 Western Road
Shoreham-By-Sea
West Sussex, BN43 5WD
England

Books

Behrned, Katrin and Wegler,
   Monika. *The Complete
   Book of Cat Care*. Barron's
   Educational Series, Inc.,
   Hauppauge, New York,
   1991.
Carlson, Delbert G., D.V.M.,
   and Giffin, James M., M.D.
   *Cat Owner's Veterinary
   Handbook*. Howell Book
   House, New York, 1983.
Helgren, J. Anne. *Abyssinian
   Cats: A Complete Pet
   Owner's Manual*. Barron's
   Educational Series, Inc.,
   Hauppauge, New York,
   1995.
Robinson, Roy. *Genetics for
   Cat Breeders*. 2nd ed.
   Pergamon Press, Oxford,
   1977.
Siegal, Mordecai and Cornell
   University. *The Cornell
   Book of Cats*. Villard
   Books, New York, 1989.
Taylor, David. *The Ultimate
   Cat Book*. Simon and
   Schuster, New York, 1989.
Taylor, David. *You & Your
   Cat: A Complete Guide to
   the Health, Care &
   Behavior of Cats*. Alfred A.
   Knopf, New York, 1986.
Wright, Michael and Walters,
   Sally, eds. *The Book of the
   Cat*. Summit Books, New
   York, 1980.

125

The Author

Ulrike Müller has many years of experience as a breeder of purebred cats, and she acts as a judge at cat shows in countries all over the world. In addition, she is the author of successful Barron's manuals for pet owners: *Longhaired Cats, The New Cat Handbook, Persian Cats,* and co-author of *Healthy Cat, Happy Cat.*

The Illustrator

Renate Holzner works as a free-lance illustrator in Regensburg, Germany. Her broad repertoire ranges from line drawings to photorealistic illustrations and computer-generated graphics.

The Photographer

The photos in this book are by Monika Wegler with the exception of Schanz, pp. 36, 44, and 45.

Monika Wegler is a professional photographer, journalist, and author of pet books. The major focus of her work in the recent years has been pet portraits and behavioral and motor studies of cats and dogs.

First English language edition published in 1997 by Barron's Educational Series, Inc.

Published originally under the title *Die Katze (Mein Heimtier)*

© 1996 by Gräfe und Unzer verlag GmbH, Munchen
English translation © 1997 by Barron's Educational Series, Inc.

All inquiries should be addressed to:
Barron's Educational Series, Inc.
250 Wireless Boulevard
Hauppauge, New York 11788

Library of Congress Catalog Card No. 96-49554

International Standard Book Number 0-8120-6595-6

Library of Congress Cataloging-in-Publication Data
Müller, Ulrike.
[Katze. English]
Cats : caring for them, feeding them, understanding them Ulrike Müller ; photographs, Monika Wegler ; drawings, Renate Holzner.
p. cm. — (The Family pet)
Includes bibliographical references (p.) and index.
ISBN 0-8120-6595-6
1. Cats. I. Title. II. Series.
SF445.M8413 1997
636.8—dc21 96-495
CIP

Printed in Hong Kong
987654321

Important Note

Cats may scratch or bite you. Have such injuries treated by a physician immediately.

It is essential that your cat gets all the necessary vaccinations and worm treatments (see pages 72 and 74); otherwise, the health of persons and animals could be affected. Some diseases and parasites can be transmitted to humans (see pages 72–79). If your cat shows symptoms of illness, it is absolutely necessary to consult a veterinarian. If you have questions about your own health, see a physician and mention that you keep a cat. There are some people who have an allergic reaction to cat hairs. If you think you or a family member may fall into that category, ask your doctor before acquiring a cat.

There is a possibility that cats will damage other people's property or even cause accidents. It is in your own interest to arrange for adequate insurance coverage. In any event, you should have a liability insurance policy.

The Cover Photos

Front Cover: Siberian cat, tabby with white (large photo); six-week-old exotic short-haired Golden Shell (small photo)

Back Cover: Eight-week-old Norwegian Forest cat, Black Tabby at play.

Norwegian Forest cat